Color Conscious

✳

Color Conscious

THE POLITICAL MORALITY
OF RACE

✳

K. ANTHONY APPIAH
AND
AMY GUTMANN

PRINCETON UNIVERSITY PRESS

PRINCETON, NEW JERSEY

Copyright © 1996 by Princeton University Press
Published by Princeton University Press, 41 William Street,
Princeton, New Jersey 08540
In the United Kingdom: Princeton University Press,
Chichester, West Sussex
All Rights Reserved

Library of Congress Cataloging-in-Publication Data

Appiah, K. Anthony.
Color conscious : the political morality
of race / K. Anthony Appiah and Amy Gutmann.
p.   cm.
Includes bibliographical references and index.
ISBN 0-691-02661-0
ISBN 0-691-05909-8 (pbk.)
1. Race awareness—United States.   2. Racism—United States.
3. United States—Race relations.   4. Afro-Americans—Race identity.
5. Whites—United States—Race identity.
I. Gutmann, Amy.   II. Title.
E185.615.A77   1996
305.8'00973—dc20   96-21573

The authors are grateful to the Tanner Trust for support of the Tanner
Lectures on Human Values, on which the essays by K. Anthony
Appiah and Amy Gutmann were based

This book has been composed in Galliard

Princeton University Press books are printed on acid-free paper and
meet the guidelines for permanence and durability of the Committee
on Production Guidelines for Book Longevity of the Council on
Library Resources

Second printing, and first paperback printing, 1998

http://pup.princeton.edu

Printed in the United States of America

3 5 7 9 10 8 6 4 2

FOR

HENRY DAVID FINDER,

MICHAEL DOYLE,

AND

ABIGAIL GUTMANN DOYLE

＊

✳ *Contents* ✳

Color Conscious

✸

Introduction: The Context of Race

✱

DAVID B. WILKINS

In 1903, W.E.B. Du Bois proclaimed that "the problem of the twentieth century is the problem of the color-line."[1] As we approach the end of the millennium, the accuracy of Du Bois's prophecy is beyond dispute. Indeed, given the bitterness of the contemporary debate over such racially charged issues as affirmative action, multiculturalism, welfare reform, and crime, it is clear that the only shortcoming of Du Bois's baleful assessment is the implication that this most American of problems might be solved in this century. Today, only someone who consciously turns his back on the multiplicity of ways that race continues both to define and divide Americans could endorse such an optimistic projection.

Not only are we as a nation destined to fail to solve the problem of the color-line in this century, but we are in danger of losing our ability even to talk about the subject intelligently. Far too often, speakers on both sides of contemporary debates about race acknowledge only half of America's complex racial legacy. Those who oppose taking race into account, for example, when awarding benefits or designing educational curricula, point to the fact that our political institutions rest on principles of individual freedom and equality that expressly deny the moral or political significance of ascriptive characteristics such as race. Echoing Justice Harlan's famous dissent in *Plessy v. Fergusson*, these advocates passionately assert that "our Constitution is color blind," and our

I am indebted to Anthony Appiah, Lawrence Blum, Jorge Garcia, Martha Minow, Dorothy Roberts, Maneesha Sinha, and David Wong for many valuable conversations about the contemporary meaning and significance of race in American culture. Anthony Appiah, Amy Gutmann, and Dennis Thompson provided insightful comments and criticisms on earlier drafts of this introduction. Needless to say, I am solely responsible for all errors and omissions.

[1] W.E.B. Du Bois, *The Souls of Black Folk*, ed. Donald Gibson (New York: Penguin Books, 1989), p. 13.

morality is as well.[2] Supporters of affirmative action or multiculturalism, on the other hand, cite the fact that Americans—frequently acting in the name of individual freedom and equality—exterminated the indigenous Native American population, kidnapped and enslaved millions of Africans, held Japanese-Americans (but not German-Americans) in internment camps during World War II, and, from 1790 to 1952, restricted legal naturalization to "white" persons. For these advocates, "color blindness" in our political and moral discourse has been little more than a smoke screen for the pervasive "color consciousness" (and, more specifically, white supremacy) that has been a dominant feature of the American saga since the Pilgrims first landed on Plymouth Rock.

Given this dual legacy, it is not surprising, as Anthony Appiah observes in his thoughtful epilogue to this volume, that so much of what is said today about race is "dishonest, confused, ill-informed, unhelpful." If we are to fare any better on Du Bois's challenge in the next century, we must create a discourse about race that acknowledges both parts of America's racial heritage.

This volume is an attempt to create such a discourse. It does so by bringing together two leading scholars and, to quote Appiah again, "passionate democrats," to ask the kind of probing and critical questions about the meaning and significance of race that are rarely addressed in our sound bite culture. Each author brings a wealth of experience and expertise to the task. Anthony Appiah has written extensively about a wide range of topics relating to African and African-American intellectual history and literary studies, ethics, and the philosophy of mind and language. Amy Gutmann is one of the country's leading scholars in the fields of democratic theory, ethics, and public education. In the essays that follow, both these accomplished authors strive to give an account of race in contemporary American society that pays due regard both to the promise of America's ideals and to its persistent failure to live up to these noble aspirations.

Appiah's essay, entitled "Race, Culture, Identity: Misunderstood Connections," explores the role of race in the formation of individual identity. His central claim is that the concept of race

[2] *Plessy v. Fergusson*, 163 U.S. 537 (1896), p. 559.

4

developed in this country neither adequately explains existing American social distinctions nor properly acts as a surrogate for culture or identity. Although America's history of racial oppression creates a role for "racial identities," Appiah concludes, if we are ever to realize the promise of individual freedom and equality embedded in the other part of our racial heritage, "we shall have, in the end, to move beyond current racial identities."

In "Responding to Racial Injustice," Amy Gutmann brings the two parts of America's racial dilemma together to provide a "color blind" argument in favor of "color consciousness" in public policy. Gutmann argues that in order to treat individuals fairly, the ultimate goal of a just society, it will sometimes be necessary to enact color conscious policies that recognize the extent to which race continues to influence the life chances of citizens. At the same time, Gutmann insists, these policies must also be consistent with the truth about color blindness that all persons, regardless of their skin color, are civic equals. Only those color conscious public policies that are both instrumentally valuable to overcoming racial injustice *and* consistent with the fundamental equality of all human beings, Gutmann concludes, are justifiable in a democracy that hopes one day to live up to its professed ideals.

Both individually and collectively, these calm and well-reasoned investigations of the practical, political, and moral significance of race are a welcome breath of fresh air in the current overheated rhetorical climate. In the balance of this introduction, however, I want to suggest that these essays are important for reasons that transcend and ultimately redefine the limitations of contemporary race talk. Questions of race and race consciousness are intimately connected with some of the deepest and most difficult moral and political issues of our times. As the titles to their respective contributions imply, both Appiah and Gutmann speak to these often neglected and frequently misunderstood connections. Moreover, what they say about these connections—and the manner in which they frame their respective inquiries—highlights the degree to which scholars and policymakers often fail to pay sufficient attention to contextual factors that plausibly affect the moral claim for race consciousness in particular circumstances. Developing ways to recognize and account for these contextual factors without undermining our commitment to universal principles of justice, I submit, is the key to solving the problem of the color-line in the next millennium.

Appiah reminds us that discussions about race inevitably presuppose some understanding of both culture and identity. For example, consider the common claim that some or all of the current racial designations—white, black, Asian, Hispanic—define groups that share a common and distinct culture. If true, this claim adds substantial weight to the argument in favor of race consciousness in many settings. Culture provides an important underpinning for both individual human flourishing and the creation of a diversity of goods that enrich the lives of members and nonmembers alike. As a result, to the extent that race is linked to culture, we have grounds for preserving racial identity separate and apart from whatever independent value racial designations may have when standing alone.

In order to evaluate this claim, however, we must first have a clear idea of what constitutes a common culture and how we might go about determining whether whatever criteria we establish are met in any particular circumstance. Only when we have crossed this threshold can we intelligently evaluate whether the cultural products that have undeniably been associated with various racial groups in American society—for example, jazz and the African-American community—demonstrate the kind of link between race and culture that the proponents of race-based cultural distinctiveness seem to suggest.

Appiah takes this threshold issue on directly. He argues that in order to constitute a common culture, there must be a wide range of "shared beliefs, values, signs, and symbols . . . not . . . in the sense that everyone in the group actually hold the beliefs and values, but in the sense that everybody knows what they are and everybody knows that they are widely held in the society." Racial groups in the United States, Appiah asserts, do not share such common beliefs and therefore are not cultural subgroups within the broader American mosaic. Nor, he insists, can cultural identity simply be ascribed to these racial identities by virtue of a process of "cultural geneticism" in which group members are presumed to share a common culture by definition.

6

Similarly, Appiah recognizes that in order to evaluate the claim that race consciousness unfairly infringes on individual autonomy, we must first have a clear idea of what "autonomy" means. He therefore prefaces his defense of a fluid notion of racial identity by rejecting two common conceptions of the self frequently invoked by advocates at polar ends of the debate about the relationship between race and identity: that there is an "authentic nugget of selfhood" just waiting to be dug out (invoked by those who see race as part of that authentic self), and the corresponding view that "I can simply make up any self I choose" (invoked by those who believe that we must be free to reject all forms of ascriptive identity). Instead, Appiah argues that "we make ourselves up" but only from a "tool kit made available by our culture and society." Although race and race consciousness are undoubtedly part of the American experience, Appiah warns that "recognizing" these aspects of our identity involves accepting "scripts" about what constitutes "a proper way of being [for example] black." Thus, Appiah concludes, despite the fact that the demand for recognition often springs from understandable, perhaps even noble origins— for example, rejecting the white racist's ascription of a set of negative characteristics to skin color in favor of a positive account of black pride—making race a central feature of identity invariably runs the risk of replacing the tyranny of racism with the tyranny of racial expectations.

Appiah's account of culture and identity is controversial, as is his application of these concepts to the current racial designations in the United States. I shall examine some of these issues presently. Whether or not one finds Appiah's conclusions persuasive, his careful treatment of these topics underscores the extent to which focusing on race and race consciousness highlights and clarifies issues central to our political morality broadly understood. Politicians and political theorists alike base arguments about such diverse topics as government funding for the arts, prayer in school, and pornography on simplistic claims about culture and identity. By forcing us to confront how race potentially problematizes these simplistic understandings, Appiah leads the way toward a more careful examination of these concepts throughout our political discourse.

Indeed, even when he speaks directly about the meaning of race, Appiah helps to clarify concepts central to our political morality. In this essay as elsewhere, Appiah trenchantly argues that in order to understand the meaning of race in contemporary discourse, we must first examine two other topics of central concern to democratic theory: linguistics and science.

To talk intelligently about race, Appiah argues, we must first understand what individuals mean when they use the term. Borrowing concepts from linguistics and the history of science, Appiah conducts a systematic investigation—a literary archeology, if you will—of the manner in which intellectual and political elites in the United States and the United Kingdom have in fact deployed the term "race" throughout the nineteenth and twentieth centuries. At the core of this account, Appiah argues, are a series of connected assertions about the inherent relationship between certain morphological characteristics of human beings (most notably skin color) and the moral, intellectual, or physical "essences" of those who display these traits. Thus, Appiah concludes, the contemporary meaning of "race" is parasitic on submerged but nevertheless powerful claims about the scientific foundations of racial divisions.

These "ideational" claims, as Appiah refers to them, are demonstrably false. Whether one focuses on Jefferson's assertion that skin color is linked to moral traits such as truthfulness or bravery, on neo-Darwinist claims about the speciation of human beings into distinct races with their own unique physical and mental traits, or on Herrnstein's and Murray's recent attempts to suggest that blacks are genetically less intelligent than whites, there simply is no credible scientific evidence to support the idea that the current racial designations in the United States capture any meaningful physical, intellectual, or moral differences among human beings who fall into these categories. As a result, Appiah concludes, there are no "races" in the United States or elsewhere as that term has come to be understood; there are only social groups that have been constructed for purposes that cannot be defended on the scientific grounds on which the modern ideational meaning of race must inevitably rest.

Once again, the importance of Appiah's careful examination of the linguistic and scientific underpinnings of race does not depend upon whether one agrees with his ultimate conclusion that there are "no races." Our public discourse about politics and morality is filled with terms like "equality," "fairness," and "efficiency," the meanings of which are at least as contested and potentially misunderstood as "race." By demonstrating how tools from linguistics and the philosophy of language can illuminate the assumptions underlying our contemporary usage of race, Appiah offers a way of further specifying the meaning of these other concepts as well.

Moreover, as our society falls ever more under the sway of technology, science is likely to play an expanding role—both explicitly and implicitly—in our political and moral lives. Already, the meanings of "life" and "death" have been powerfully transformed by assumptions about what science can or cannot achieve. In the not too distant future, scientific breakthroughs in the fields of genetic engineering and computer technology are likely to challenge many of our assumptions about individuality, merit, deliberation, and a host of other concerns that are fundamental to how citizens will live, work, and interact with each other in a twenty-first-century democracy. Appiah's careful exposition of the scientific underpinnings of race is an important blueprint for how we might evaluate the claims of science in these new realms.

Amy Gutmann's essay is equally rich in insights that underscore the connection between race and our political morality. How a democracy should respond to racial injustice depends upon our understanding of what "justice" requires when individuals have been denied the right to equal citizenship on the basis of their race. As Gutmann's thoroughgoing analysis makes clear, the answer to this question depends in turn on our understanding of morality, law, and ultimately politics.

Gutmann's critique of the common assertion that public policy concerning race should be evaluated by moral principles that would be suitable to a just society is an important case in point. Those who claim that the government can respond to racial injustice only by adhering to strict principles of color blindness and nondiscrimination frequently justify their position by pointing to the broad consensus among philosophers and ordinary citizens that in an ideal society benefits and burdens would not be distributed on the basis of race. Despite its superficial appeal, this

9

argument, as Gutmann points out, fails to account for the fact that America in the last decade of the twentieth century is far from a just society. Color blind policies treat individuals fairly when racism and other forms of disadvantage based on color no longer affect the lives of citizens. But when color continues to exert a major influence on the ability of citizens to participate equally in public and private life, as it surely does in the United States, color conscious policies may be the only way to accord individuals the fair treatment that is their moral due. Fairness, not color blindness, Gutmann insists, is the fundamental principle of justice by which public policies must be judged in the nonideal world.

This framework has important implications for moral argument that extend far beyond the question of responding to racial injustice. If political philosophy is to guide us in the real world, then its practitioners must begin to elaborate the moral principles that ought to govern public policy in a society beset by many kinds of injustice. To be sure, in order to uncover these principles, we must first have an understanding of what justice would require in an ideal world. And there may be good reasons for society to reject a policy, no matter how justified as a response to present injustice, that moves us too far from the conditions that would allow us to bring this ideal world into being. But applying "just" policies in a setting where these conditions have not been met will often produce "unjust" results. As Gutmann rightly points out, the circumstances in which this is likely to be true, and therefore the degree to which ideal principles must be modified to take account of nonideal realities, cannot be identified in the abstract. Thus political philosophy must pay more attention to the social, economic, and political forces that perpetuate injustice in American society. By highlighting the extent to which racial injustice is created and reinforced, Gutmann underscores the need for a more contextual and fact-specific approach to political theory.

Gutmann's account also sheds important light on the relationship between this approach to political theory and the legal doctrines that articulate and preserve the rights of citizens. Gutmann draws on two legal cases to illustrate her contention that color blindness is not the uniquely appropriate response to racial injustice: the first involves the Piscataway, New Jersey, school board's use of race as a tie-breaking criterion in deciding to lay off a white teacher instead of a black teacher with equal seniority; the second involves a constitutional challenge to a North Carolina voting district constructed for the sole purpose of guaranteeing a black majority. By using these examples, Gutmann highlights the extent to which in the American political system, principles of justice are often crafted in the context of constitutional litigation. Although she is careful to note that law and morality are not identical, she nevertheless insists that Justice Harlan's famous injunction that "the Constitution is color blind" is parasitic on the same ideal theory claim that presents color blindness as a fundamental moral imperative in the first instance. To the extent that this latter claim fails because it does not account for the injustices of our nonideal world, the assertion that color blindness is central to constitutional analysis must also be rejected.

Gutmann's analysis of the role of moral argument in legal decision-making, however, does not stop with the traditional (albeit certainly important) observation that we should not interpret the Constitution to express a political morality at odds with our general moral convictions. Instead, because she insists that principles of justice must speak to the actual conditions in which we live, she also stakes a claim for the role of moral argument in interpreting the factual context within which legal mandates are applied. Thus in the Piscataway case, much of the force behind the white teacher's claim that she was treated unfairly (as opposed to the simple claim that she lost out because of a color conscious governmental decision) comes from the assertion that she was denied a job for which she was "equally qualified" solely on the basis of race. Most commentators who have discussed this case treat the issue of qualifications as a purely factual question and assume without discussion that having met the relevant standard, the white teacher had a right not to be deprived of her position for reasons other than "merit" or "unavoidable bad luck."

Gutmann rejects this simple syllogism. Assessing the white teacher's qualifications, she insists, is a moral as well as a factual inquiry, as is the determination of whether any qualified individual has a right to a particular job. Both what counts as a "qualification" and the acceptable criteria for selecting among those who meet the relevant standard are social constructions that depend in large measure on the social purposes that society seeks to achieve

11

by filling a particular job. Deciding on what these purposes are and how they should be ranked is a normative inquiry, subject to principles of justice. In a world in which race affects virtually every aspect of both a candidate's life chances and her ability to perform a given job, this inquiry is unlikely to be color blind.

Gutmann's analysis, therefore, underscores the fact that judges should pay attention to moral arguments in two distinct places in their analysis: first, when choosing principles to interpret the meaning of ambiguous legal provisions, and second, when evaluating factual claims about how those provisions should be applied. This way of understanding the role of moral argument in law challenges a number of widely held assumptions about the general relationship between law and morality. Textualism, originalism, and positivism all seek to draw a sharp line between these two spheres. If, as Gutmann implies, morality requires that judges consult moral principles when both "finding" and "applying" legal rules, then we must develop a richer account of how judges can take these considerations into account in a manner that supports traditional rule of law values such as equality, predictability, and democratic accountability.

Neither general principles of justice (even when modified to fit our nonideal world) nor morally informed Constitutional jurisprudence can provide a full answer to how we should respond to racial injustice. This is true for two reasons. First, in the vast majority of cases, both moral principles and constitutional decisions are likely to leave considerable room for individual variation. Second, because we are concerned with policies that will be applied in the real world, the fact that some responses to racial injustice are likely to garner more support than others is a relevant criterion for choosing among them. Politics, as opposed to moral theory or law, is therefore likely to play the biggest role in shaping our actual responses to racial injustice.

In light of her previous work, it should come as no surprise that Gutmann's analysis of the politics of race also illuminates the general relationship between morality and politics. I will touch on only three of these insights here. First, by carefully examining the argument that we should substitute class consciousness for race consciousness, Gutmann reminds us that moral arguments both bound and shape the legitimate domain of public opinion. Although class consciousness may very well be morally justified given the economic inequality in American society, it is not a morally sufficient answer to the problems addressed by race conscious policies for the simple reason that race is an independent source of disadvantage. Moreover, since what is popular among citizens depends in part on what officials say about the moral foundations of public policy, the instrumental argument in favor of "class, not race"—that it is more palatable to whites—is in one important respect circular and therefore of dubious weight in forming a political morality that seeks to guide us rather than simply reflect prevailing prejudices.

Second, Gutmann argues that the fact that citizens are unwilling to adopt policies that would effectively address racial injustice is itself an additional moral reason for preserving those policies that, although arguably less effective, have already been adopted. Thus the moral claim underlying the popular objection that affirmative action programs primarily benefit middle-class blacks while improving the fortunes of poor blacks only indirectly is substantially undercut by the public's unwillingness to enact programs, such as broad, economically based reparations that would benefit poor blacks directly.

Third, by analyzing the Supreme Court's decisions in two recent voting rights cases, Gutmann underscores how the morality of the results of an electoral process are relevant to the morality of the process itself. In each case, the Supreme Court questioned a redistricting plan that was designed to create majority-black districts in areas where blacks had been unable to influence electoral results because of racial block voting. In reaching these results, a majority of the Court assumed that the only justification for creating these districts was to ensure that the number of blacks elected to Congress is proportionate to their numbers in the voting population. This rationale, the Court concluded, is unconstitutional because it assumes that all blacks share the same political interests and will prefer the same candidates.

Gutmann offers an alternative rationale. Although giving black voters greater chance for electoral success may increase the number of black elected representatives, it also will allow blacks (regardless of whether they elect a black to represent them) to exert more influence over the substance of the legislative agenda.

Since blacks, as a matter of contingent historical circumstances, are more likely than whites to place overcoming racial injustice at the top of their list of legislative priorities—a moral good for all citizens—society has good reason to favor voting schemes that increase black electoral success separate and apart from whatever values are associated with increasing the number of black legislators.

Each of these arguments has important applications outside of the context of responding to racial injustice. The relationship between moral argument and public opinion, the moral force underlying second-best public policies, and the moral connection between results and process are all central to the democratic project. Focusing on the challenge that race consciousness poses for democracy simply brings these issues into sharp relief.

Both these essays therefore shed light on a broad array of issues that are crucial to forging a political morality capable of leading us into the next century. When we turn our attention back to issues of race, however, the sheer breadth of the topics addressed in this volume gives rise to an additional, and as yet largely unexplored, set of questions about the role of context in moral arguments about race. Once we acknowledge that thinking about race helps us to understand concepts as diverse as culture, science, and politics, it is fair to ask whether the unique features of each of these realms has any bearing on the meaning or moral significance of race consciousness in these different domains. If the answer to this question is yes, as both Appiah and Gutmann seem to imply, then what is the relationship between this contextualized understanding of race and our general theoretical and practical commitment to universalism in our moral and political discourse?

We can begin to get a sense of these problems by noting the inevitable tension created by the fact that both authors appear to embrace a different answer to the question Appiah poses—what should be the role of race in individual identity?—from the one that they endorse with respect to Gutmann's query about whether it is morally acceptable for the government to implement race conscious public policies. Like Appiah, Gutmann believes that races are nothing more than a social construct masquerading as scientific fact. She therefore argues that we should talk about "color consciousness" instead of "race consciousness" as a way of symbolizing our rejection of the claim that race should play a central role in individual identity. For his part, Appiah agrees with Gutmann that "government *can't* be color blind, because society isn't." Notwithstanding that there are, in fact, "no races," many Americans continue to act as if there are—in ways that disproportionately disadvantage the members of some racial groups. A government committed to norms of equality and freedom, Appiah agrees, ignores this reality at its peril.

These two positions are not inherently inconsistent. To the contrary, when taken together, I believe that Appiah and Gutmann make a compelling case both that fairness requires that the government recognize the ways in which race continues to influence the life chances of individuals and that individuals should not view their own or their fellow citizens' identities as being, to borrow Appiah's phrase, "too tightly scripted" by race. Nevertheless, these two spheres cannot be entirely separated. In a society committed to individual liberty and mutual respect, we depend upon our democratic institutions to foster a social world in which free and equal citizens can enjoy the fruits of our rich cultural heritage. One cannot advocate color consciousness (or color blindness, for that matter) in public policy without examining how this choice is likely to affect this ultimate goal—just as it would be equally wrong to form judgments about culture and identity that ignored the political consequences of these important choices.

Given this interdependence, we must confront a host of difficult questions if we are to advocate that government should take one stance toward race and individuals another. For example, what message is conveyed to individuals about their own identities when government distributes benefits and burdens on the basis of race? Or, to ask the question from the opposite perspective, what are the implications for concerted political action by oppressed minorities when we downplay the role of race in individual identity?

Both authors give us important clues about how we might begin to address these concerns. With respect to the first issue, Gutmann's insistence that all race conscious government policies should both reduce injustice and satisfy the color blind criteria

15

of fairness helps citizens to understand that it is justice, and not simply race, that underlies color consciousness in public policy. Similarly, Appiah concedes that it may be "historically [and] strategically necessary" for members of oppressed groups to construct "positive" scripts about their racial identity as a means of combating negative stereotypes and mobilizing their members for effective political action. Once we accept that governments and individuals ought at least in some circumstances to treat race and race consciousness differently, elaborating these and other similar insights about the moral and practical interdependence of these two spheres must become a priority for those interested in the political morality of race.

Moreover, once we acknowledge that context does play a legitimate role in moral arguments of this kind, we must consider whether differences *within* the domains of public policy and individual identity plausibly affect our considered judgments about the morality of race consciousness. Within the sphere of public policy, for example, we might ask whether the social purposes underlying particular institutions affect the moral argument for race consciousness, and how various color conscious *and* color blind criteria relate to those purposes. As Amy Gutmann points out, before one can characterize a particular instance of race consciousness as "preferential treatment," one must first examine whether race is a legitimate qualification for the position. This in turn is a function of the "social purposes" for which the position was created. These social purposes, however, differ considerably by context.

Consider the argument, eloquently defended by Gutmann, that being black is a legitimate credential for university admissions. The strength of this argument depends upon how we conceive of our goals for higher education. Contrary to the tone of much of the rhetoric surrounding the repeal of affirmative action at the University of California, the most plausible account of the social purpose of higher education is not that it is a prize for those with the best high school records and test scores. Even if we concede that these criteria measure a certain kind of valuable intellectual ability, society legitimately expects more from universities than simply giving students with these talents an opportunity to enhance their skills. At a minimum, society expects universities to produce a new generation of citizens capable of assuming a broad range of leadership roles. In a society as diverse (and as racially polarized) as our own, in order to meet this goal, universities must provide, in Gutmann's terms, "identity" and "diversity" role models so that students of all races can both see that people like themselves can succeed and learn the value of interacting with people who are different.[3] Indeed, a strong argument can be made that a university system that failed to educate a fair percentage of students from any significant social group in society, no matter how "justified" on the basis of criteria such as grades and test scores, would have defaulted on its primary duty to ensure the preservation of a stable polity, since the kind of entrenched inequality that would inevitably result from such a state of affairs is fundamentally corrosive to democratic values.

These goals, however, are arguably less central to other institutions where race conscious policies might be applied. Although we might believe that many public employers—police departments, for example—have a social responsibility to promote democratic values similar to the academy's, we do not generally hold private employers to this same level of commitment. Thus, to take an example with which I am familiar, the goal of ensuring an educated citizenry is at best of only secondary importance to law firms when they select new members; the primary qualifications relate to a new recruit's ability to deliver services to clients competently, efficiently, and ethically. Even in these settings, race may be a bona fide qualification for other reasons: consider a law firm that hires a Korean-American lawyer to open the firm's new office in Seoul, Korea. Nevertheless, without more, the argument that firms ought to hire "identity" or "diversity" role models stands on substantially different footing from the argument that universities ought to do so. Although these goals can certainly be used to break ties between candidates of equal qualifications, to elevate black candidates (even those who meet the threshold qualifications for the position) over white candidates with higher qualifications is to engage in "preferential treatment" that must be

---

[3] Harvard president Neil Rudenstine has recently issued a major report defending this view: *The President's Report 1993–1995* (Cambridge: Harvard University, 1996).

justified on grounds that rest outside the social purposes of the institution (for example, breaking down racial stereotypes or compensating for past injustice).

Before one evaluates the merits of these other justifications, however, it is important to realize that the standard for judging whether a particular example of preferential treatment is justified depends upon how closely the existing color blind criteria actually fit the social purposes that the position was designed to serve. In cases where the criteria for measuring good job performance are uncontroversial and easily observable, we would expect this fit to be quite close. Imagine a professional basketball team drafting college players or a skilled carpenter evaluating a new apprentice on the basis of a sample of her work. In many circumstances, however, a combination of the subjectivity of quality assessments and the fact that those who are being hired have yet to develop the skills and dispositions that the employer is seeking make it likely that the fit between credentials and social purposes will be relatively loose. Once again, consider the law firm. Although the kind of intelligence and hard work captured by law school grades and test scores undoubtedly are valuable to legal employers, no one has ever demonstrated that these signals are closely correlated with the skills and dispositions that are likely to make someone a competent, efficient, and ethical practitioner. The looser the fit between these "color blind" criteria and the social purposes of the job, the less force there is to the claim that departing from these criteria to achieve some other social purpose (for example, breaking racial stereotypes) violates the rights of either those who are not selected or, more important, those who ultimately use the service.

Social purpose is also central to the moral case for color consciousness at the level of individual decision-making. Both Appiah and Gutmann recognize that there is an important moral difference between the use of race as a tool of oppression and the way in which historically oppressed groups have traditionally used various forms of ascriptive identity including race as a means of rallying together to provide mutual support and to fight their unjust treatment. This distinction is not based on the claim that those who are linked together by racial injustice have an inherent commitment to fighting oppression. To ascribe virtue to oppressed

18

minorities is to buy into the same false ideas about racial "essences" that, as Appiah's essay conclusively demonstrates, helped to create the oppression in the first place. Instead, as Gutmann argues, color blind principles of fairness and reciprocity dictate that individual members of an oppressed group should not free ride on efforts by other group members to end their mutual oppression. These principles also give whites a moral reason to be color conscious, both in the sense of recognizing how racism has injured blacks and other minorities and, perhaps even more important, by acknowledging the extent to which whites have been the beneficiaries (whether intentional or not) of a host of advantages as a result of this nation's legacy of racial injustice.

In this context as well, however, the strength of this moral claim depends upon how closely the actions that are taken in the name of fairness "fit" the social purpose of eliminating racial injustice. Those who advocate racial solidarity as a means of fighting injustice confront two dangers that, if ignored, threaten to undermine the moral value of this strategy. On the one hand, unless we pay close attention to the consequences of the actions taken under this banner, solidarity and mutual aid can easily slide into simple cronyism or, worse yet, an attitude that oppressed people are incapable of oppressing others. On the other hand, if we develop too fine a notion of the "proper" way for minorities to respond to racial injustice, we run the risk, to borrow from Appiah again, of scripting these lives too tightly in a manner that will not only infringe on individual autonomy but also runs the risk of undermining the struggle against racism by silencing dissent and debate within the minority community.

To negotiate this moral Scylla and Charybdis, we must begin to develop a more nuanced understanding of how individuals can "fit" their actions into the struggle for racial justice without undermining either the rights of others or their own unique moral personality. Often this will involve deciding how to balance three distinct kinds of moral claims. The first, which is the primary focus here, stems from the fact that in our nonideal society, race matters in ways that plausibly affect moral decision-making. The second results from the fact that those who must decide how they will take race into account frequently occupy social roles—lawyers, public servants, university officials—that also constrain moral decision-making. Finally, as Appiah reminds us, we are more than the sum total of our racial and role obligations. A moral theory that will not, as Appiah cautions, substitute the tyranny of racial expectations for the tyranny of oppression must provide space for individual expression and flourishing.

Once again, deciding how to balance these three claims in any particular case requires that we pay careful attention to context. This includes considering the factors that bear on how particular circumstances affect the strength of each of the three moral claims. We must also assess the decision-making context as well. Thus it is one thing to suggest how an individual might balance the legitimate pull of these three moral domains; it is another to claim that people who disagree with this balance have a right to impose sanctions on those they believe have reached the wrong conclusion. The latter, while certainly sometimes justified, poses a far greater threat to individual autonomy.

Context therefore plays a potentially important role in our understanding of the morality of color consciousness both between the spheres of public policy and individual decision-making and within each of these domains. Just as in the former analysis regarding differences between the "public" and the "private" sphere, acknowledging contextual differences within each of these arenas must be the beginning and not the end of the analysis. Even if we believe that the overall morality of public policy would be improved if we made the kind of distinctions about "purpose" and "fit" that I have advocated, we must still investigate the long-term consequences of the government applying different criteria for judging race conscious policies in, for example, educational institutions from those in law firms. Similarly, individuals need guidance about how to balance the competing demands of the various aspects of their moral identities in particular cases. Once again, those interested in the political morality of race must begin to grapple with these pressing problems.[4]

[4] For my own tentative attempts to elaborate these ideas in the context of the obligations of black lawyers, see David B. Wilkins, "Social Engineers or Corporate Tools: *Brown v. Board of Education* and the Conscience of the Black Corporate Bar," in *Brown at Forty*, ed. A. Sarat (Oxford: Oxford University Press, 1996); Wilkins, "Race Ethics and the First Amendment: Should a Black Lawyer Represent the Ku Klux Klan?" *George Washington Law Review* 63 (August

Finally, there are other arguably relevant contextual factors that cut across the loose public/private distinction that has occupied my attention up to this point. Consider, for example, distinctions among groups. Is the moral significance of racial identity the same for all those groups that are recognized as "races" in American society? Appiah and Gutmann implicitly give different answers to this increasingly important question. Throughout his essay, Appiah speaks broadly about all forms of racial identity, at times specifically linking his conclusions about race to other nonracial but nevertheless ascriptive identities such as gender and sexual orientation. Gutmann, on the other hand, explicitly limits her discussion to African-Americans. Both these approaches raise intriguing questions.

Appiah's collective treatment of all forms of ascriptive identity is consistent with the dominant discourse of both conservatives, who tend to see all these assertions of identity as equally problematic, and liberals, who frequently speak of "minorities" (or even more broadly of "minorities and women") as if the arguments in favor of race consciousness were equally applicable to all disadvantaged groups. Given that all these groups share many common experiences of oppression and define themselves at least in part in terms of their opposition to white male supremacy, it is not surprising that the bearers of these marginalized identities have tended to be drawn to each other and to be treated with collective disdain by those in positions of power. Nevertheless, there are good reasons to believe that the contingent experiences of these various groups do affect the morality of race consciousness in both what I have been calling the private and the public spheres.

Consider the relationship between race and culture. As Appiah's definition of culture implies, self-consciousness about group membership and values are key factors in determining whether individuals who have been grouped together for some purposes share a common culture. White Americans have never had this kind of self-awareness. With the exception of white su-

---

1995): 746–86; and Wilkins, "Two Paths to the Mountaintop? The Role of Legal Education in Shaping the Values of Black Corporate Lawyers," *Stanford Law Review* 45 (1993): 1981–2026.

premacists and the most committed white multiculturalists, white Americans rarely see themselves as "raced" at all. Nor, unlike members of other racial groups, have they been forced to adopt a racial identity in response to systematic state supported racial prejudice. For most whites, therefore, their culture is "American culture," or, even more unselfconsciously, simply the way things are. Given these social realities, to speak of whites as sharing a common culture based on race makes little sense.

Nor is it likely that the diverse range of peoples who have been lumped together under the label "Asian" or "Hispanic" share a common culture in any morally significant way. Virtually all the peoples who have been crammed together under these labels have a national or subnational culture—Japanese, Chinese (including Cantonese, Hakkanese, etc.), Korean, Vietnamese, and so on—with which they strongly identify. These national identities come complete with language and other cultural symbols that are as distinct from one another as they are from mainstream American culture. Indeed, many of these national homelands (for example, Japan and Korea) have harbored resentments and antagonisms toward one another dating back hundreds of years. Consequently, the assertion that despite all these differences a third generation descendant of a Chinese aristocrat shares a common culture with a Vietnamese boat person in any meaningful sense lacks credibility.

Black Americans, on the other hand, have had a very different experience. Unlike whites, blacks cannot forget for one minute that they have a race; a race that links each individual black to the fate of every other black. Whether one takes the casual racism of the cab driver who refuses to pick up a black man on the assumption that he is a criminal, or the sophisticated "statistical discrimination" of employers who judge individual blacks by the mean achievement levels of all blacks, black Americans know that their individual chances for achieving success in America are linked to the advancement of the race as a whole. As a result, blacks have looked to each other for both mutual protection and the kind of love and support that is essential to human flourishing. Not surprisingly, this process has produced distinctive styles and modes of expression, attitudes and beliefs about political and social issues, customs and practices, that are recognized and understood (if not always agreed with or followed) by a broad range of blacks across geographic and social lines.

Nor do black Americans, unlike the vast majority of "Asians" and "Hispanics," have any alternative cultural frame of reference within which they feel either embraced or nurtured. Although many blacks now refer to themselves as African-American, this identification is as much (if not more) of a social construct than race. Despite the fact that at least some of the ancestors of virtually every black American can be traced to Africa, as Appiah himself has noted in another context, any common culture that may have existed between the descendants of African slaves and their African forebears has long ago been destroyed, first by the concerted efforts of slave owners, and, more important, by the passage of time.[5] Thus while black Americans can *claim* African culture, we have never had the luxury of *relying* on our African heritage to provide a set of common symbols and beliefs within which we can organize our lives. This history separates African-Americans from every other group of hyphenated Americans.

To be sure, what I am now calling "black culture" has not developed independently of what I referred to a moment ago as "American culture." As Appiah concisely notes, "African-American identity . . . is centrally shaped by American society and institutions: it cannot be seen as constructed solely within African-American communities." But this does not mean that African-American cultural identity is *the same as* American identity, even though Americans of all races have surely helped to shape its many parameters. Hip-hop, support for affirmative action, pride in Colin Powell's (and yes, even Clarence Thomas's) accomplishments—and shame for the atrocities committed by Colin Ferguson—the rage unleashed in the L.A. riots, and the claim that the police framed O.J. are all recognized and understood, although certainly not embraced or endorsed, by a broad range of black Americans in ways that differ significantly from the way that these styles, attitudes, and beliefs are understood by whites.

---

[5] See Kwame Anthony Appiah, *In My Father's House: Africa in the Philosophy of Culture* (New York: Oxford University Press, 1992).

Whether or not this suffices to prove that black Americans share a "common culture" in the terms that Appiah describes, it underscores that race plays a different role in the formation of African-American cultural identity than it does for other racial groups.

A similar argument in favor of paying attention to differences among racial groups applies in the public arena as well. Consider once again the argument that "class, not race" should become the guiding force behind public policy. This argument implicitly trades on the notion that "class" has the same meaning for all groups in American society. Social science research, however, consistently demonstrates that this is simply not true. William Julius Wilson and other prominent scholars have marshalled an impressive array of data calling attention to growing class divisions within the black community.[6] Nevertheless, as Michael Dawson cogently argues in an important new book, middle-class blacks differ in several important respects from their white counterparts.[7] For example, on average, black middle-class households are one-third poorer than white middle-class households. They depend to a far greater extent than whites on two paychecks. Moreover, this income must go farther, because middle-class blacks are much less likely to come from middle-class families and therefore often end up supporting other family members as well as themselves. As a result, white families earning $10,000 a year have as much accumulated wealth (in terms of net assets) as black families earning $50,000.

In addition, the black middle class tends to be concentrated in sectors of the economy that make it particularly vulnerable. Unlike their white counterparts, middle-class blacks are most likely to be employed in either the manufacturing or government sectors—two areas that have been (and are likely to continue to be)

[6] See William Julius Wilson, *The Declining Significance of Race* (Chicago: University of Chicago Press, 1980); and William Julius Wilson, *The Truly Disadvantaged: The Inner City, the Underclass, and Public Policy* (Chicago: University of Chicago Press, 1987).

[7] See Michael C. Dawson, *Behind the Mule: Race and Class in African-American Politics* (Princeton: Princeton University Press, 1994). Unless otherwise indicated, the following statistics and comparisons were all culled from Dawson's excellent book.

hard hit by changes in the American economic and political systems. Even the members of the new black professional class, whom the advocates of "class, not race" continually single out as not deserving "preferential treatment," are much more dependent on the kind of activist government that is increasingly under attack in American politics than are their white counterparts. At the most basic level, professional blacks depend upon the government to vigorously enforce the antidiscrimination laws that give these pioneers a fighting chance to overcome the racism that undeniably still exists in American society. For many black professionals, however, the connection runs even deeper. Affirmative action programs, government set-asides, the rise of black political power in major urban areas, and the higher visibility of public procurement decisions have all combined to create important opportunities for black professionals in fields such as law, investment banking, construction, and financial services. As a result, even those black professionals who work in the most prestigious jobs in the private sector often depend on the government for a substantial portion of their income and, as a consequence, for their survival.

The cumulative result of all these factors is that the black middle class is far more marginal and vulnerable than the picture painted by the advocates of "class, not race" would lead one to suspect. Black middle-class workers are nearly twice as likely as their white counterparts to become unemployed.[8] Indeed, throughout the 1980s, the black middle class lost many of the gains (both as an absolute matter and relative to whites) that it had achieved during the previous three decades.

This reality is directly relevant to both the fairness and the efficacy of substituting class for race in public policy. Are the children of precarious black middle-class households really so undeserving of programs that recognize that they face greater obstacles to carrying their middle-class status into the next generation than similarly situated whites? Is it sound public policy to destabilize the fledgling black middle class by removing one of its primary means

---

[8] See Walter L. Updergrave, "Race and Money," in *Money*, December 1989, p. 152.

of support? These questions become visible only when we stop looking at "class" as a monolithic concept that operates in the same way for all groups.

Indeed, there are good reasons to suspect that class differences are less meaningful for blacks than they are for other minorities in the United States. One typical way in which middle-class families solidify their status is by moving into a better neighborhood, thereby gaining access to better schools and other public facilities, safer streets, and the myriad other benefits that flow from associating with successful people. Given that whites continue to make up the vast majority of middle-class households, this generally means moving to an integrated community. Blacks, however, are far less likely to live in such communities than any other racial group. As Douglas Massey and Nancy Denton report in their massive study of segregation in American society, "The high level of segregation experienced by blacks today is not only unprecedented compared with the experience of European ethnic groups: it is also unique compared with the experience of other large minority groups, such as Asians and Hispanics."[9] Blacks are more than twice as isolated as members of both these other groups, who are more likely to share a neighborhood with whites than with members of their own group. Even those blacks who have moved to the suburbs are likely to be concentrated in racially segregated towns or neighborhoods, and therefore cut off from many of the benefits of integration.[10] In a world in which one's residence is highly correlated with a broad range of economic, social, and cultural factors, this pattern is certain to make it more difficult for middle-class blacks to translate their income into other forms of capital upon which middle-class success ultimately rests. Once again, this reality is relevant to any public policy that seeks to distribute benefits on the basis of class.

The fact that middle-class status means something different for blacks from what it means for other groups should come as no surprise. Although blacks, Hispanics, Asians, gays and lesbians, and physically disabled persons (to name just a few) have all been

[9] Douglas S. Massey and Nancy A. Denton, *American Apartheid: Segregation and the Making of the Underclass* (Cambridge: Harvard University Press, 1993), p. 67.

[10] Ibid., pp. 67–74.

discriminated against, each group's history is unique. Take the kind of racial stereotypes that are deployed against the members of various groups. Throughout American history, blacks have been portrayed as lazy, stupid, dirty, licentious, and prone to criminal behavior. Without in any way minimizing the damage that has been done, for example, to Asian-Americans by being typecast as "the model minority," these specific stereotypical images of blacks seem particularly likely to inhibit black economic success in a way that cuts across class lines. Studies of educational and workplace experience that disaggregate data by race support this conclusion.[11] These differences are morally relevant to a public policy that uses economic success as a surrogate for disadvantage. Once again, we are likely to see this point only if we pay careful attention to distinctions among groups.

Recognizing that various racial groups may have different moral claims for race conscious public policy or for giving race a more prominent place in individual decision-making, however, creates its own distinctive problems. Amy Gutmann carefully states that by limiting her analysis to blacks she is not claiming that blacks are the only group currently suffering from the "systematic instantiation of racial injustice in the United States." Nevertheless, by focusing on the unique concerns of black Americans she—and I—run the risk of minimizing the problems of other groups that also cry out for redress. Indeed, if we are not careful, the proponents of context run the risk of creating a culture of victimhood in which different groups compete for benefits and status on the ground that their suffering is more intense or authentic than that felt by other groups.

More important, as America becomes an increasingly multiracial society, one can legitimately ask whether it is possible to discuss responding to injustice against blacks without considering the impact that race conscious public policies will have on other racial minorities. To cite only one prominent example, the recent

---

[11] See Lewis A. Kornhauser and Richard L. Revesz, "Legal Education and Entry into the Legal Profession: The Role of Race, Gender, and Educational Debt," *New York University Law Review* 70 (1995): 829–964; and "Subcommittee on Retention of the Committee to Enhance Minorities in the Profession, Report on the Retention of Minority Lawyers in the Profession," reprinted in *The Record* 48 (1992): 355.

controversy involving a challenge by some Asian-Americans to a desegregation order that allocates by race places in a prestigious California high school dramatically underscores the additional complexity in the moral argument for race consciousness that is introduced once one moves away from a world in which there are only blacks and whites.[12] Are Asian students treated fairly by a policy that, although admittedly designed to remedy past injustices against blacks, also makes it substantially more difficult to overcome racial injustice against them?

Without question, this case and others like it raise difficult problems for a political morality that directs our attention to distinctions among disadvantaged groups. Once we acknowledge that these distinctions are both real and morally significant, however, the solution cannot be that we should act as though group differences do not exist. Instead, we must press further to determine how the context of multiracialism affects the moral weight that should be attached to any group's, or indeed any individual's, invocation of race consciousness in public policy and individual decision-making.

Our success in grappling with these complex questions ultimately depends upon the strength of our commitment to democratic values in general and reasoned deliberation in particular. For anyone familiar with the many instances in which these values have failed us—particularly with respect to issues concerning race—this may seem like an admission of defeat. But just as America must acknowledge both parts of its complex racial heritage if we are to make progress on the problem of the color-line in the coming century, those of us who have been disappointed by this nation's repeated unwillingness to extend the promise of democracy and freedom to blacks and other racial minorities must never

[12] See Selina Dong, "'Too Many Asians': The Challenge of Fighting Discrimination against Asian Americans and Preserving Affirmative Action," *Stanford Law Review* 47 (1995): 1027–57 (noting that 85 percent of the students in San Francisco's unified school district are minorities, of which 65 percent are Asians); and Deborah Ramirez, "Multicultural Empowerment: It's Not Just Black and White Anymore," ibid., pp. 957–92 (noting that in 1990, only 50 percent of the minority population in the United States was black—down from 96 percent in 1960).

lose faith in this flawed system that nevertheless remains, to paraphrase Winston Churchill, better than all the available alternatives.

Like Appiah and Gutmann, I too am a passionate democrat even though I understand that there has never been a moment in America's democratic experiment that has not been thoroughly tainted by racism and other forms of oppression. I draw strength in this conviction from the fact that, despite his clear-eyed understanding of America's problems, Du Bois never lost his faith either in the "great watchwords of liberty and opportunity" that form the core of this nation's democratic ideals or in the ability of reasoned deliberation to bring us closer to realizing these noble aspirations. Appiah closes his epilogue to this volume by quoting Du Bois's commitment to these uniquely American ideals, no matter how tarnished and neglected. I can think of no more fitting way to close this introduction to a book grounded in the faith that reasoned deliberation among people of good will constitutes our best hope of solving in this century, the problem Du Bois so eloquently set out for the last, than to repeat the words that Du Bois himself used to close his own valiant attempt to spark such a dialogue:

> HEAR MY CRY, Oh God the Reader; vouchsafe that this my book fall not still-born into the world-wilderness. Let there spring, Gentle One, from out its leaves vigor of thought and thoughtful deed to reap the harvest wonderful. . . . Thus in Thy good time may infinite reason turn the tangle straight, and these crooked marks on a fragile leaf be not indeed THE END.[13]

[13] Du Bois, *The Souls of Black Folk.*

Race, Culture, Identity:
Misunderstood Connections

✳

K. ANTHONY APPIAH

PART 1. ANALYSIS: AGAINST RACES

Explaining Race Thinking

IMAGINE yourself on Angel Island in the 1920s. You are helping an inquisitive immigrant from Canton to fill in an immigration form. *Name*, it says. You ask her name. She tells you. You write it down. *Date of birth*. She gives it to you (according to the Chinese calendar, of course, so you have to look up your table for translating from one system to another). Then there is an entry that says *Race*. This you do not have to ask. You write "Oriental." And your interlocutor, because she is inquisitive, asks politely: "What are you writing now?" (After all, until now, everything you have written has been in response to her answers.)

Disingenuously, you say: "I am writing down where you are from."

"Ah yes," she replies helpfully, "Canton, I was born in Canton. How did you know?"

I should like to express my sense of enormous indebtedness to Lawrence Blum, Jorge Garcia, Martha Minow, Richard T. Ford, Maneesha Sinha, David Wilkins, and David Wong, for discussions both together and separately; to Houston Baker and Lucius Outlaw for prompting me (in Lucius's case, regularly!) to rethink these issues; to many people, whose names I have not recorded, to whom I have talked about identity and culture at many universities over the last few years; to several generations of students in my Introduction to Afro-American Studies class at Harvard; and, above all, to Henry Finder, on whom I try out most of my ideas first. I delivered a Tanner lecture on these issues at the University of California at San Diego in 1994, and the occasion provided the first stimulus for me to bring these thoughts together; the very helpful responses of many who responded there helped in the preparation of this more extended version of my thoughts. Naturally, responsibility for the opinions expressed here remains mine alone.

"No. Actually, that's the next question I was going to ask. Place of birth."

"So what have you written already?"

How do you answer this question? Seventy years ago, how would you have explained to someone from outside the modern West what our English word "race" meant? Or how would you have explained to a Sicilian across the continent on Ellis Island, thirty years earlier, why the right answer for him was "Caucasian"? (Where he came from, the people of the North of Italy, the ancestors of the modern Lombard league, think of him, as he very well knows, as of a different, darker, *razza* than theirs: how do you explain that here he is going to become white?) And would you give the same explanation today?

Or, again, imagine yourself in North Carolina, in the later nineteenth century, as Reconstruction is coming to an end. You are in a small town, out of the way, where there are families that come in all shades of skin color, milk through chocolate. A message comes through from the state capitol in Raleigh. Everyone now has to be white or colored. If you're white, step this way; colored, go the other. You are talking to Joe, a teenager, whose skin is milky white, whose eyes are blue, but whose grandmother, Mary, is a brown-skinned woman who remembers *her* mother's stories of Africa. "I was gonna go with my grandma," he tells you. "But then I saw my Uncle Jim was gonna be with her, so I'm gonna cross to the other side of the room. 'Cause one thing I know for sure; I don't want to be anywhere my Uncle Jim's gonna be."[1]

Is Joe making a conceptual mistake? Or is he unintentionally making what will turn out to be a lucky choice for him and his descendants; a choice that will leave him and them with a vote, better schools, better jobs? Can you imagine someone like Joe, in the nineteenth-century South, born after emancipation but raised before the high-water mark of the strange career of Jim Crow, who doesn't know that in America, or at least in the Carolinas, even white-skinned people with black grandmothers are Negroes?

My preliminary aim in this essay is to explore the concept of race that is at work in these cases—an American concept, though

---

[1] I owe this thought experiment to a conversation with Samuel R. Delany.

also, of course, one that draws on and interacts with ideas from elsewhere. I will go on to argue for three analytical conclusions. First, I want to explain why American social distinctions cannot be understood in terms of the concept of race: the only human race[2] in the United States, I shall argue, is *the* human race. Second, I want to show that replacing the notion of race with the notion of culture is not helpful: the American social distinctions that are marked using racial vocabulary do not correspond to cultural groups, either. And third, I want to propose that, for analytical purposes, we should use instead the notion of a racial identity, which I will try to explore and explain.

Finally, I will argue for an ethical conclusion: that there is a danger in making racial identities too central to our conceptions of ourselves; while there is a place for racial identities in a world shaped by racism, I shall argue, if we are to move beyond racism we shall have, in the end, to move beyond current racial identities.

Meaning

If in the 1920s you'd left Angel Island and traveled much farther east than Ellis Island, sailing across to England, landing at Southampton and taking the train up to London and on to Cambridge, you could have consulted the leading experts in the English-speaking world on questions of meaning. In 1923 Charles K. Ogden and I. A. Richards had published *The Meaning of Meaning: A Study of the Influence of Language upon Thought and of the Science of Symbolism*, with supplementary essays by various people including the anthropologist Bronislaw Malinowski. A year earlier Ludwig Wittgenstein had published the *Tractatus Logico-Philosophicus*, which was to become a classic in a field that was not yet called the philosophy of language.

We do not need to delve deeply into that field. But it will help us later, when we turn to some of the difficult philosophical ques-

---

[2] I'm going to avoid my normal custom of using scare-quotes around the word "race" throughout, because in this context it would be question begging. It would also be confusing, since a lot of what I have to say is about the alleged relation between the word "race" and allegedly actual races. So quotes around the word "race" in this piece are for the purposes of distinguishing between use and mention.

tions about understanding the idea of race, if we make a distinction that was already available when Wittgenstein was writing the *Tractatus*.

Before I introduce that distinction, however, I want to draw attention to the fact that the issues I am going to be discussing next grow out of a tradition of philosophical reflection that is not directly concerned with ethical matters. It is particularly important, I think, to illustrate how technical philosophy can be of the greatest help in clarifying our moral predicament; and to show that what can be helpful lies as much in the spheres of metaphysics and epistemology and philosophy of language as it does in the field of ethics. Now to the theoretical distinction.

In the 1920s there were—and there are still today—two very different and competing philosophical notions of what it is to give an adequate account of the meaning of a word or expression.

One—we can call this the "ideational" view of meaning—which goes back to at least the seventeenth century and the Logic of Port Royal, associates the meaning of a term, like "race," with what the Port Royal Logicians called an "idea." Understanding the idea of race involves grasping how people think about races: what they take to be the central truths about races; under what sorts of circumstances they will apply the idea of race; what consequences for action will flow from that application.

The other picture of meaning—the "referential" view—suggests that to explain what the word "race" means is, in effect, to identify the things to which it applies, the things we refer to when we speak of "races."

These views are not as far apart as they might at first appear. To find out what people are referring to in using the word "race," after all, you might need to know what idea their word "race" expresses: if they had no ideas, no thoughts, about race, and if there were no circumstances when they used the word, no consequences to their applying it, then we could hardly suppose that their making the sound "race" meant anything at all. In practice, at least, access to an idea of race is probably needed to find the referent.

And, conversely, once we have identified the referent—found, that is, the races—we can assume that people who understand the word "race" have some beliefs that are at least roughly true of races. For if people are talking about races, it is because they have, or think they have, experience of races: and, generally speaking, some of that experience will be reliable. A little bit of knowledge of what races are like combined with a little information about what people are like—how sensory experience works, for example—will allow us to predict at least some of people's ideas about races.

My aim is not to decide between these two broad traditions of conceiving of meaning. Anyone concerned to understand our concept of race ought, I think, to be interested both in the reality of race and in the way people think about it, in both the referential and the ideational aspects: we can leave it to the philosophers of language to wrangle about which of these ought to have the central place in semantics (or whether, as I suspect, we need both of them).

The Ideational Account of Race

Perhaps the simplest ideational theory of meaning runs like this: what we learn when we learn a word like "race" is a set of rules for applying the term. Everybody who knows what the word "race" means—which means most competent speakers of English—learns the same rules: so that while people have different beliefs about races, they share some special beliefs—I'll call them the criterial beliefs—that define the concept. These beliefs may not be very high-powered. They might include, for example, the thought that people with very different skin colors are of different races or that your race is determined by the race of your parents. But on this simplest ideational theory, all these criterial beliefs have this property: someone who doesn't believe these things doesn't understand what the English word "race" means.

The simplest theory would also require that if we collected together all these criterial beliefs about race and took them all together, they could be thought of as defining the meaning of the word "race." (This is equivalent to saying that there are things that have to be true of something if it is to be a race—conditions necessary for being a race; and that these necessary conditions are, when taken together, sufficient for being a race.) We can use a device invented by the English philosopher Frank Ramsey in the 1920s to make this an explicit definition: something is a race just in case all the criterial beliefs are true of it.[3] Let's call this the "strict criterial theory."

The Ramsey definition makes clear the connection between defining a term and questions of existence: there are races if, but only if, there are things that satisfy all the criteria.

For a number of reasons, which again I want to skirt, you won't get many philosophers of language to buy into this strict criterial theory today; there is a general skepticism about it, which goes back, I suppose, to W.V.O. Quine's attack on the idea of the analytic truth, which he called one of the "dogmas of empiricism." For if the strict criterial theory were right, those criterial sentences would be analytically true: they would be sentences that were true simply by virtue of their meanings, and Quine urged us to doubt that there *were* any of those.[4]

But you don't need highfalutin semantic arguments to be lead to wonder whether we could in fact write a Ramsey-style definition of the word "race." Consider each of the two claims I gave a little while ago. *People with very different skin colors are of different races. Your race is determined by the race of your parents.*

Take the first one. Suppose Jorge were to speak of the Latino "race" and to maintain that the whole range of colors found among people that the U.S. census would classify as Hispanic simply demonstrated that a race didn't have to be fairly monochrome. Is this a mistake about the meaning of the word "race"? Now take the second claim. Two people marry. The wife has one Ghanaian and one British parent. The father's parents are Norwegian. They have children of various shades, one of whom looks, to all intents and purposes, like an average Norwegian. My friend Georg agrees that the mother's parents are of different races and contends that the Norwegian-looking son is Caucasian, but his darker brothers are not. Does Georg not know what "race"

---

[3] See "Theories," in Frank Ramsey, *Foundations: Essays in Philosophy, Logic, Mathematics and Economics*, ed. D. H. Mellor (London: Routledge and Kegan Paul, 1978), pp. 101–25.

[4] W.V.O. Quine, "Two Dogmas of Empiricism," in *From a Logical Point of View* (Cambridge: Harvard University Press, 1953), pp. 20–46.

means? Apparently, if people with two parents of the same race are of the same race as their parents. For if your race is determined by the race of your parents, you must have the same race as your full siblings.

It seems to me simply unconvincing to insist that Jorge and Georg don't know what the word "race" means; at least if knowing what it means is knowing whatever you need to know to count as a competent user of the English word "race." This fails, of course, to establish that we couldn't find a set of beliefs necessary and sufficient for understanding the word "race"; beliefs, that is, that everybody who understands the word "race" must have and such that everybody who has them understands the concept of race. But if even *these* rather uncontroversial-looking claims turn out to be ones that can be denied by someone who understands the word "race," then one might begin to wonder whether *any* claims will turn out to be necessary: and if none are necessary, then certainly the conjunction of the necessary conditions won't be sufficient.

Such doubts about the strict criterial theory—in terms of criteria individually necessary and jointly sufficient—lead us on to the next obvious proposal, one that might seem to be suggested by Wittgenstein's use of the notion of a criterion.[5] Perhaps what is required to know what "race" means is that you should believe most of the criterial beliefs (or a good number of them) but not that you should believe any particular ones. The explicit definition that captures the common notion of those who understand the word "race" will then be given by a modified Ramsey-style definition: a race is something that satisfies a good number of the criterial beliefs. I'll call this the "vague criterial theory."

Accepting this theory has certain important consequences. First of all, it isn't going to allow us to draw a sharp line between not knowing what the word "race" means and having unusual views about races. That boundary is vague, because the expression "a good number" is vague.

Second, the theory admits that among the criterial beliefs are

[5] See P. F. Strawson, "Wittgenstein's Conception of a Criterion," in *Wittgenstein and the Problem of Other Minds*, ed. Harold Morick (Brighton, Sussex: Harvester Press, 1981).

some that are plainly not held by everybody who uses the word "race." For example, *Most sub-Saharan Africans are of the Negro race. Most Western Europeans are of the white race. Most Chinese are of the yellow race. Everybody has a race. There are only a few races.*

There are clearly people who count as understanding the term "race" who don't believe each of these things. Somebody who uses the word "race" may have no thoughts at all about Africa or Western Europe or China, need not know even that they exist. I, as you will see, deny that everybody has *a* race, because I think nobody has a race: but there are more moderate folks who think that people of so-called mixed race are neither of the race of their parents nor of some separate race and deny that everybody has *a* race for that reason.[6] And there have been physical anthropologists who felt that the only useful notion of race classified people into scores of kinds.

If the strict criterial theory had been true, it would have been easy to argue against the existence of races. One would only have had to find the correct definition and then show that nothing in the world actually satisfied it. This looser theory correspondingly makes it harder to argue against the existence of races. But the vague criterial theory does suggest a route to understanding the race concept: to explore the sorts of things people believe about what they call "races" and to see what races would have to be like for these things to be true of them. We can then inquire as to whether current science suggests that there is anything in the world at all like *that*.

Now, suppose there isn't one such thing in the world; then, on this view, there are no races. It will still be important to understand the vague criteria, because these will help us to understand what people who believe in races are thinking. That will be important, even if there are no races: first, because we often want to understand how other people are thinking, for its own sake; and second, because people act on their beliefs, whether or not they are true. Even if there are no races, we could use a grasp of the vague criteria for the concept of race in predicting what their

[6] See Naomi Zack, *Race and Mixed Race* (Philadelphia: Temple University Press, 1993).

thoughts and their talk about race will lead them to do;[7] we could use it, too, to predict what thoughts about races various experiences would lead them to have.

I have already declared myself very often on the question whether I think there are any races. I think there aren't. So it is important that I am clear that I also believe that understanding how people think about race remains important for these reasons, even though there aren't any races. To use an analogy I have often used before, we may need to understand talk of "witchcraft" to understand how people respond cognitively and how they act in a culture that has a concept of witchcraft, whether or not we think there are, in fact, any witches.

The ideational view might, therefore, lead you to explore contemporary thought and talk about races. But I think—remembering Jorge and Georg—that this is likely to produce a confusing picture. This is because current ways of talking about race are the residue, the detritus, so to speak, of earlier ways of thinking about race; so that it turns out to be easiest to understand contemporary talk about "race" as the pale reflection of a more full-blooded race discourse that flourished in the last century. The ideational theory can thus be combined with a historical approach: we can explore the ideational structures of which our present talk is, so to speak, the shadow, and then see contemporary uses of the term as drawing from various different structures, sometimes in ways that are not exactly coherent.

Before we turn to historical questions, however, let me ask what route to understanding the race concept is suggested by the referential account of meaning.

The Referential Account of Race: Philosophy of Science

The answer is most easily understood by thinking about an issue in the history and philosophy of science. From the point of view of current theory some previous theories—early nineteenth-cen-

[7] Strictly speaking, if there aren't any races, there's no talk or thought about races. So this is a shorthand for "talk they would assent to (or thoughts they would express) using the word 'race' and its cognates."

38

tury chemistry, say—look as though they classified some things—acids and bases, say—by and large correctly, even if a lot of what they said about those things was pretty badly wrong. From the point of view of current theory, you might argue, an acid is, roughly, a proton donor.[8] And our recognition of the fact that the classification of acids and bases was in itself an intellectual achievement is recorded in the fact that we are inclined to say that when Sir Humphrey Davy—who, not having any idea of the proton, could hardly be expected to have understood the notion of a proton donor—used the word "acid," he was nevertheless talking about what we call acids.

The issues here are at the intersection of the philosophy of language and the philosophy of science. And in explaining why it seems proper to think that Sir Humphrey Davy was referring to the things we call "proton donors," even though much of what he believed about acids is not true of proton donors, philosophers of science have borrowed ideas about reference from recent philosophy of language.

One proposal some have borrowed is what is called the "causal theory of reference." The idea is simple enough: if you want to know what object a word refers to, find the thing in the world that gives the best causal explanation of the central features of uses of that word. If you want to know what the name "New York" refers to, find the object in the world that is at the root of most of the causal chains that lead to remarks containing the expression "New York."

So in the case of acids, we are urged to believe that the stuffs "out there" in the world that really accounted for the central features of Davy's "acid"-talk really were acids and that that is what accounts for our sense that Davy was not simply talking about something else (or, of course, about nothing at all). Early physiologists (like Descartes) who talked about "animal spirits" in the nerve fibers, on the other hand, we now say were referring to nothing at all: there is no currently recognized stuff that can account for what they said about animal spirits; instead there are truths about sodium pumps and lipid bilayers and synapses. There

---

[8] This is the so-called Bronsted theory of the Danish physical chemist Johannes Nicolaus Bronsted.

simply is no substance that was usually present when and only when the expression "animal spirits" was uttered and that behaves at all as they thought animal spirits behaved.

The Referential Account of Race:
A Proposal

How can we use these ideas to develop a referential account of the concept of race? Well, we need to explore the sorts of things people have said about what they call "races" and see whether there is something in the world that gives a good causal explanation of their talk. If there *is* one thing in the world that best explains that talk, then that will be what the word "race" refers to; and that can be true, even if it would surprise most people to know that that was what they were really talking about—just as Sir Humphrey Davy would have been surprised to discover that when he said "acids," he was talking about—referring to—proton donors.

As a practical matter, at least three things are required for us to allow that a past theorist who spoke of Ys and was badly mistaken was nevertheless talking about *some*thing, call it X.

First, the existence condition—*we* must acknowledge the existence of X.

Second, the adequacy condition—*some* of what was thought to be true of what Y denoted must be at least approximately true of X.

Third, the uniqueness condition—X must be the best candidate for the job of Y's referent, so that no other thing that satisfies the existence condition satisfies the adequacy condition equally well.

On the causal theory, what it is for X to be the best candidate for the job of Y's referent in the speech of a community is for X to be the thing that best causally explains their talk about Ys. So what we need to do, on this view, is explore the history of the way the word "race" has been used and see if we can identify through that history some objective phenomenon that people were responding to when they said what they said about "races."

The difference between ideational and referential theories of meaning, then, is roughly that the referential theory requires that we do a historical version of what the ideational theory permits us to do. On the referential theory, exploring the history of the term is central to understanding what it means. Semantical considerations thus steer us toward historical inquiry.

A Note on Method

The history I am going to explore is the history of the ideas of the intellectual and political elites of the United States and the United Kingdom. You might ask why I don't look at the words of more ordinary people: race is statistically most important in ordinary lives. A good question, I say. (This is what you say when you think you have a good answer.) The reason is itself embedded in the history: as we shall see, throughout the nineteenth century the term "race" came increasingly to be regarded, even in ordinary usage, as a scientific term. Like many scientific terms, its being in use among specialists did not stop its being used in everyday life. Treating it as a scientific term meant not that it was only for use by scientists but that scientists and scholars were thought to be the experts on how the term worked. That is, with the increasing prestige of science, people became used to using words whose exact meanings they did not need to know, because their exact meanings were left to the relevant scientific experts.

In short, there developed a practice of *semantic deference*: people used words like "electricity" outside the context of natural philosophy or physical science, assuming that the physicists could say more precisely than they could what it meant. This semantic deference thus instituted a new form of what Hilary Putnam has called "linguistic division of labor," just as older specialties, like theology or law, had for a long time underwritten concepts— the Trinity, landlord—whose precise definition ordinary people didn't know.

The result is that even ordinary users of the term "race," who operated with what I have called vague criteria in applying it, thought of themselves as using a term whose value as a tool for speaking the truth was underwritten by the experts. Ordinary users, when queried about whether their term "race" really referred to anything, would have urged you to go to the experts: the medical doctors and anatomists, and later, the anthropologists and philologists and physiologists, all of whom together developed the scientific idea of race.

This makes the term "race" unlike many other terms in our language: "solid," for example. "Solid" is a term that we apply using everyday criteria: if I tell you that materials scientists say that a hunk of glass is not a solid but a liquid, you may well feel that they are using the term in a special technical sense, resisting semantic deference. Some people might want to defend the word "race" against scientific attacks on its legitimacy by denying, in effect, that semantic deference is appropriate here. Of this strategy, I will make just this observation: if you're going to go that route, you should probably offer some criteria—vague or strict—for applying the term. This is because, as we shall see, the arguments against the use of "race" as a scientific term suggest that most ordinary ways of thinking about races are incoherent.

Thomas Jefferson: Abolitionist

The understandings of "race" I am exploring are American; it seems appropriate enough, then, to begin with a thinker who helped shape the American republic: namely, Thomas Jefferson. And I want to begin with some representative reflections of his from the first quarter of the nineteenth century; for it is in the nineteenth century, I think, that the configuration of ideas about race we have inherited began to take its modern shape.

In Thomas Jefferson's *Autobiography*—begun, as he says, on January 6, 1822, at the age of seventy-seven—the third President of the United States reproduces his original draft of the Declaration of Independence, with the passages deleted by the Congress "distinguished by a black line drawn under them."[9] There are only two paragraphs entirely underlined in black; and the second, and by far the longer of them, gives, as grounds for complaint against "the present king of Great Britain,"[10] the fact that "he has

---

[9] *Autobiography*, in Thomas Jefferson, *Writings* (New York: Library of America, 1984), p. 18.
[10] Ibid., p. 21.

waged cruel war against human nature itself, violating its most sacred rights of life and liberty in the persons of a distant people who never offended him, captivating & carrying them into slavery in another hemisphere, or to incur miserable death in their transportation thither. This piratical warfare, the opprobrium of INFIDEL powers, is the warfare of the CHRISTIAN king of Great Britain."[11] This first failure at gathering the new republic around the banner of antislavery did not discourage him. Not many pages later, Jefferson reports his equally unsuccessful attempts to persuade the legislature of Virginia to proceed, albeit gradually, toward total emancipation: "But it was found that the public mind would not yet bear the proposition, nor will it bear it even at this day. Yet the day is not distant when it must bear and adopt it, or worse will follow. Nothing is more certainly written in the book of fate than that these people are to be free."[12] So far, I think, we can feel that Thomas Jefferson was not simply ahead of his times, at least in the state of Virginia, but that, allowing for changes in rhetorical taste, he is our moral contemporary.

The sentence that follows disrupts this happy illusion: "Nor is it less certain," the former President writes, "that the two races, equally free, cannot live in the same government."[13] For Jefferson, who offers here no defense of his view, this is a piece of common sense. Here is a point at which we see one of the central characteristics of Jefferson's way of thinking about race: *it is a concept that is invoked to explain cultural and social phenomena*, in this case, the alleged political impossibility of a citizenship shared between white and black races.

Thomas Jefferson: Race Theorist

If we want to know the sources of Jefferson's stern conviction— "Nor is it less certain . . ."—we can turn to Query XIV of the *Notes on the State of Virginia*, published four decades earlier, in the 1780s. Emancipation is inevitable, Jefferson has argued; and it is right. But blacks, once emancipated, will have to be sent elsewhere. Jefferson anticipates that we may wonder why, especially

[11] Ibid., p. 22. [12] Ibid., p. 44.
[13] Jefferson, *Autobiography*.

given "the expence of supplying, by importation of white settlers, the vacancies they will leave."

> Deep rooted prejudices entertained by the whites; ten thousand recollections, by the blacks, of the injuries they have sustained; new provocations; the real distinctions which nature has made; and many other circumstances, will divide us into parties, and produce convulsions which will probably never end but in the extermination of the one or the other race.—To these objections, which are political, may be added others, which are physical and moral. The first difference which strikes us is that of colour. Whether the black of the negro resides in the reticular membrane between the skin and scarf-skin, or in the scarf-skin itself; whether it proceeds from the colour of the blood, the colour of the bile, or from that of some other secretion, the difference is fixed in nature, and is as real as if its seat and cause were better known to us. And is this difference of no importance? Is it not the foundation of a greater or less share of beauty in the two races? Are not the fine mixtures of red and white, the expressions of every passion by greater or less suffusions of colour in the one, preferable to that eternal monotony, which reigns in the countenances, that immoveable veil of black which covers all the emotions of the other race? Add to these, flowing hair, a more elegant symmetry of form, their own judgment in favour of the whites, declared by their preference for them, as uniformly as is the preference of the Oranootan for the black woman over those of his own species. The circumstance of superior beauty, is thought worthy attention in the propagation of our horses, dogs, and other domestic animals; why not in that of man?[14]

Apart from this difference of color, with its attendant aesthetic consequences, Jefferson observes that there are other relevant differences: blacks have less hair on their face and bodies; "they secrete less by the kidnies, and more by the glands of the skin, which gives them a very strong and disagreeable odour"; "they seem to require less sleep. . . . They are at least as brave and more adventuresome. But this may perhaps proceed from a want of forethought." (Jefferson has forgotten the Aristotelian proposal that bravery is *intelligent* action in the face of danger.) "They are

---

[14] *Notes of the State of Virginia* (1781–82), in Jefferson, *Writings*, p. 264.

more ardent after their female; but love seems with them to be more an eager desire, than a tender delicate mixture of sentiment and sensation. Their griefs are transient."[15]

> Comparing them by their faculties of memory, reason, and imagination, it appears to me, that in memory they are equal to the whites; in reason much inferior, as I think one could scarcely be found capable of tracing and comprehending the investigations of Euclid; and that in imagination they are dull, tasteless, and anomalous. . . . [Among African-Americans] some have been liberally educated, and all have lived in countries where the arts and sciences are cultivated to a considerable degree, and have had before their eyes samples of the best works from abroad. The Indians, with no advantages of this kind, will often carve figures on their pipes not destitute of design and merit. . . . They astonish you with strokes of the most sublime oratory; such as prove their reason and sentiment strong, their imagination glowing and elevated. But never yet could I find that a black had uttered a thought above the level of plain narration; never see even an elementary trait of painting or sculpture. In music they are more generally gifted than the whites with accurate ears for tune and time, and they have been found capable of imagining a small catch. . . . Misery is often the parent of the most affecting touches in poetry.—Among the blacks is misery enough, God knows, but no poetry. . . . Religion indeed produced a Phyllis Whately [*sic*]; but it could not produce a poet. The compositions published under her name are below the dignity of criticism.[16]

Jefferson has nicer things to say about Ignatius Sancho, an African whose letters had been published in London in 1782.[17] And the judiciousness of his tone here adds, of course, greatly to the weight of his negative judgments. A little later in the same long paragraph—it is nearly six pages in the Library of America edition—he writes: "Whether further observation will or will not verify the conjecture, that nature has been less bountiful to them in the endowments of the head, I believe that in those of the heart

---

[15] Ibid., p. 265.   [16] Ibid., p. 206.
[17] Ignatius Sancho (1729–80), *Letters of the Late Ignatius Sancho, an African* (London: printed by J. Nichols, 1782).

she will be found to have done them justice. That disposition to theft with which they have been branded, must be ascribed to their situation, and not to any depravity of the moral sense."[18] Though he tells us that "the opinion, that they are inferior in the faculties of reason and imagination, must be hazarded with great diffidence,"[19] he nevertheless concludes:

> I advance it as a suspicion only, that the blacks whether originally a distinct race, or made distinct by time and circumstances, are inferior to the whites in the endowments both of body and mind. It is not against experience to suppose, that different species of the same genus, or varieties of the same species, may possess different qualifications. Will not a lover of natural history then, one who views gradations in all the races of animals with the eye of philosophy, excuse an effort to keep those in the department of man as distinct as nature has formed them. This unfortunate difference of colour, and perhaps of faculty, is a powerful obstacle to the emancipation of these people.[20]

After so conspicuously fair and balanced a discussion, it would have been hard not to share Jefferson's "suspicion." His very caution here adds to rather than detracting from the force of his conclusions; and after so much attention to the "difference . . . of faculty," it is easy to miss the fact that Jefferson believes that Negroes and whites must be kept apart, even if his "suspicion" is mistaken. For Jefferson the political significance of race begins and ends with color.

Jefferson's claims here about the Negro's faculties went neither unnoticed nor unanswered. And we can find, in his letters as in the *Notes*, evidence that he remained willing to entertain the possibility that his skepticism about the capacities of the Negro was unwarranted. In a letter of August 30, 1791, to Benjamin Banneker, who had worked on the design of the Capitol in Washington—he was one Negro gentleman who was certainly capable of "comprehending the investigations of Euclid"—Jefferson wrote: "No body wishes more than I do to see such proofs as you exhibit, that nature has given to our black brethren, talents equal to

---

[18] Jefferson, *Notes of the State of Virginia*, pp. 268–69.
[19] Ibid., pp. 269.   [20] Ibid., pp. 270.

those of the other colors of men, and that the appearance of want in them is owing merely to the degraded condition of their existence, both in Africa & America."[21] And he repeats the sentiment in a letter to Henri Grégoire. Thanking the Abbé for sending him a copy of his *La littérature des nègres* (1808) Jefferson writes:

> Be assured that no person living wishes more sincerely than I do, to see a complete refutation of the doubts I have myself entertained and expressed on the grade of understanding allotted to them by nature, and to find that in that respect they are on a par with ourselves. My doubts were the results of personal observation [one wonders, a little, about the Orangutan here] on the limited sphere of my own State, where the opportunities for the development of their genius were not favorable, and those of exercising it still less so. I expressed them therefore with great hesitation; but whatever be their degree of talent it is no measure of their rights. Because Sir Isaac Newton was superior to others in understanding, he was not therefore lord of the person or property of others.[22]

The Enlightenment Idea

I have quoted so much of Jefferson in part, of course, because Jefferson is an important figure in the history of American debates about racial politics; but mostly because in these passages I have cited we see something entirely representative of the best thinking of his day: the running together of biology and politics, science and morals, fact and value, ethics and aesthetics. Jefferson is an intelligent, sensitive, educated American shaped by the Western intellectual currents we call the Enlightenment: if we query these conflations, we are querying not so much an individual as the thinking of a whole culture.

Let us explore the structure of Jefferson's explanation of why black and white races cannot live together in equality and harmony. He begins with suggestions that do not especially rely on the character of the race concept: prejudice, on the part of whites,

[21] August 30, 1791, to Benjamin Banneker. "Letters," in Jefferson, *Writings*, p. 982.
[22] February 25, 1806, to Henri Grégoire. Ibid., p. 1202.

and justified resentment, on the part of blacks. But almost immediately he moves on to speak of "the real distinctions which nature has made." And the first of these "physical and moral" differences is the primary criterion for dividing the black from the white race: skin color. Notice that in a passage devoted to a sociopolitical question—let me repeat that the issue here is why the races can't live together in harmony—he spends a great deal of time on theories about skin color and its consequences for the physiology of the expression of the emotions. Notice, too, however, that Jefferson holds the dark skin color and the nature of Negro hair to be relevant in part because they mean that whites are of "superior beauty" to blacks; an argument that appears to presuppose that beauty is a condition for fraternity; or, even—something that the passage hints at rather than asserting—that men can share citizenship with other men only if they find each other's women sexually attractive. I think we can assume that if Jefferson had seen that either of these premises was implicit in his argument, he might well have rejected (especially the second of) them: my point is only that it requires some such assumption to make his observations genuinely relevant to the question at hand.

Jefferson continues to talk about physical matters and their aesthetic consequences—hairlessness, kidneys, sweat—before moving on to discuss questions of the moral character of the Negro—bravery, lustfulness, crudeness of feeling (no "tender, delicate mixture of sentiment and sensation"), shallowness (those transient griefs)—and ends, at last, with the intellectual capacities—or rather, incapacities—of black people.

This passage is representative of late eighteenth-century discussions of race because, as I say, it brings together considerations that we are likely to think should be kept distinct. Remember always why the intellectual incapacity of blacks—their inferior reason—is invoked: not to justify unequal treatment—Jefferson, the democrat, clearly believes that intellectual superiority does not warrant greater political power, superior rights—but as part of a catalog of differences, which, taken together, make it certain that blacks and whites cannot live together as fellow citizens.

And it is clear that Jefferson believes that the answer to this question lies in what we would call differences in physiology, and moral and cognitive psychology, distinctions that, if they are real, we too are likely to regard as "distinctions which nature has made."

Not only, then, is race, for Jefferson, *a concept that is invoked to explain cultural and social phenomena*, it is also grounded in the physical and the psychological natures of the different races; it is, in other words, what we would call a *biological concept*.

From Natural History to Race Science

I say that it was what *we* would call a biological concept, because the science of biology did not exist when Jefferson was writing the *Notes*.[23] What did exist was natural history; and Jefferson would have agreed that race was a natural historical notion, as much as was the idea of species that Linnaeus had developed and which Buffon had popularized.[24] To think of race as a biological concept is to pull out of the natural history of humans a focus on the body—its structure and function—and to separate it both from mental life—the province of psychology—and from the broader world of behavior and of social and moral life. If Jefferson's discussion, with its movement from questions of the morphology of the skin, to discussions of sexual desire, to music and poetry, strikes us as a hodgepodge, it is because we live on the other side of a great intellectual chasm, which opens up with increasing speed through the nineteenth century. For we live now with a new configuration of the sciences; and, more especially, with the differentiation from the broad field of natural history, of anatomy, physiology, psychology, philology (i.e., historical linguistics), sociology, anthropology, and a whole host of even more specialized fields that gradually divided between them the task of describing and understanding human nature.

---

[23] "The term 'biology' first appeared in a footnote in an obscure German medical publication of 1800. Two years later it again appeared, apparently independently, and was given ample publicity in treatises by a German naturalist (Gottfried Treviranus) and a French botanist turned zoologist (Jean-Baptiste de Lamarck)." William Coleman, *Biology in the Nineteenth Century: Problems of Form, Function and Transformation*, Cambridge History of Science Series (Cambridge: Cambridge University Press, 1971), p. 1.

[24] Carolus Linnaeus, *Systema Naturae*, in which people are classified as Homo sapiens, appears in 1735.

Jefferson's discussion is representative of a transition in the way the word "race" is used in reflecting on the characters of different kinds of peoples: the outer manifestations of race—the black skin of the Negro, the white skin and round eyes of the European, the oval eyes of the Oriental—have taken their place for him besides other, less physical, criteria, in defining race. The race of a person is expressed in all these ways, physical, moral, intellectual: they are referred back, so to speak, to a common cause or ground.

Before Natural History

If we look back, for a moment, to the seventeenth-century traditions of English thought that are Jefferson's background, we see a different configuration of ideas, in which the physical body was important not as a cause but as a *sign* of difference.[25] Remember Othello. As G. K. Hunter has well expressed the matter:

> Shakespeare has presented to us a traditional view of what Moors are like, i.e. gross, disgusting, inferior, carrying the symbol of their damnation on their skin; and has caught our over-easy assent to such assumptions in the grip of a guilt which associates us and our assent with the white man representative of such views in the play— Iago. Othello acquires the glamour of an innocent man that *we* have wronged, and an admiration stronger than he could have achieved by virtue plainly represented.[26]

This device works only if the audience accepts that the Moor is *not*, simply by virtue of his Moorish physical inheritance, incorrigibly evil. Othello's blackness is a sign of his Moorishness; and it can associate him, through that sign, with the Infidel (since, unlike the Moor of Venice, most Moors are not Christian) and thus with moral or religious evil.

[25] For more on the background here see Hugh B. MacDougall, *Racial Myth in English History: Trojans, Teutons, and Anglo-Saxons* (Hanover, N.H.: University Press of New England, 1982); and Reginald Horsman, *Race and Manifest Destiny: The Origins of American Racial Anglo-Saxonism* (Cambridge: Harvard University Press, 1981).

[26] George K. Hunter, "Othello and Race-Prejudice," in *Dramatic Identities and Cultural Tradition: Studies in Shakespeare and His Contemporaries* (Liverpool: Liverpool University Press, 1978), pp. 45–46.

A similar point applies to the treatment of "the Jew" in both Shakespeare's *Merchant of Venice* and Marlowe's *Jew of Malta*. When Shylock, in what is surely his best-known speech, asks "Hath not a Jew eyes?" he is insisting that his body is a human body: and thus *essentially* the same as the body of a Gentile. He claims a status that depends on accepting that whatever is distinctive about him it is not his physical descent; what we would call his biological inheritance. So too, when Barabas in Marlowe's play is faced, by the Governor of Malta, with the accusation that Christ's blood "is upon the Jews," he replies:

> But say the Tribe that I descended of
> Were all in general cast away for sin,
> Shall I be tried by their transgression?[27]

Barabas here makes the essentially Christian point that sin and righteousness are individual matters; that they are precisely not inherited from "the Tribe that I descended of." If Barabas deserves punishment, it must be for something *he* has done: and, in fact, the Governor's reply demonstrates a grasp of this point. For he asserts that the issue is not Barabas's *descent* but his Jewish *faith*: the issue, therefore, cannot be conceptualized as simply racial. This is (a religious) anti-Judaism, not (a racial) anti-Semitism (which is, of course, not much consolation for Barabas).

There is good reason, then, to interpret these Elizabethan stereotypes, which *we* might naturally think of as rooted in notions of inherited dispositions (that is, of biology), as having much more to do with the idea of the Moor and the Jew as infidels; unbelievers whose physical differences are signs (but not causes or effects) of their unbelief.

But while Jefferson has thus moved toward conceiving of racial difference as both physical and moral, he is not yet *committed* to the view that race explains all the rest of the moral and social and political matter that is drawn into the portrait of the Negro in the *Notes*. The letters to Banneker and Grégoire reveal a man who leaves open—at least in theory—the possibility "that nature has given to our black brethren, talents equal to those of the other

---

[27] Christopher Marlowe, *The Jew of Malta* (London: Methuen, 1987), lines 340–42.

colors of men"; and throughout the *Notes* Jefferson writes with real affection and respect about Indians, who "astonish you with strokes of the most sublime oratory; such as prove their reason and sentiment strong, their imagination glowing and elevated." The differences between whites and Indians, for Jefferson, hardly constitute a difference of essential natures.

If we move on another fifty or so years from Jefferson's *Autobiography*, we enter once more a new intellectual landscape: one in which there is no longer any doubt as to the connection between race and what Jefferson calls "talent": and here, of course, the word "talent"—deriving from the New Testament parable of the talents—refers to inherited—to "native"—capacities.

Matthew Arnold:
On the Study of Celtic Literature

Let me turn, then, from Jefferson and move on into the second half of the nineteenth century, to the work of a poet and critic who, like Jefferson, uses the concept of race to explain the moral and the literary but, unlike him, is convinced that biological inheritance helps determine every aspect of racial capacity: Matthew Arnold.

Arnold was the greatest English critic of the nineteenth century. He was also a central Victorian poet, an influential essayist, and a lecturer: in short, a very public intellectual, whose influence was extended into the United States, not least by his lecture tour here in 1883 to 1884 (in his early sixties) which lead to the publication, in 1885, of *Discourses in America*.

In 1857 Matthew Arnold was elected to the Professorship of Poetry at Oxford, a position he held for about a decade. Ten years later, he published a series of lectures he had given as Professor of Poetry, *On the Study of Celtic Literature*. Arnold begins with a somewhat melancholy description of a visit to an Eisteddfod—a festival of Welsh bards—in Llandudno in North Wales. On an "unfortunate" day—"storms of wind, clouds of dust, an angry, dirty sea"[28]—Arnold sits with a meager crowd listening to the last representatives of a great poetic tradition performing for a small

[28] Matthew Arnold, *On the Study of Celtic Literature and on Translating Homer* (New York: MacMillan, 1883), p. 6.

audience in a language he admits he does not understand. ("I believe it is admitted," Arnold observes drily, "even by admirers of Eisteddfods in general, that this particular Eisteddfod was not a success."[29])

This sad episode is only the preliminary, however, to an argument for the view that the ancient literature of the Celts—of Ireland and Wales, in particular—is part of the literary heritage of Britain; even of those Britons in England who by then conceived of themselves as heirs to a Saxon heritage and were inclined, by and large, to hold the Irish Celts, in particular, in less than high regard.

Here is how Arnold makes his case:

> Here in our country, in historic times, long after the Celtic embryo had crystallised into the Celt proper, long after the Germanic embryo had crystallised into the German proper, there was an important contact between the two peoples; the Saxons invaded the Britons and settled themselves in the Britons' country. Well, then, here was a contact which one might expect would leave its traces; if the Saxons got the upper hand, as we all know they did, and made our country be England and us be English, there must yet, one would think, be some trace of the Saxon having met the Briton; there must be some Celtic vein or other running through us. . . .
>
> Though, as I have said, even as a matter of science, the Celt has a claim to be known, and we have an interest in knowing him, yet this interest is wonderfully enhanced if we find him to have actually a part in us. The question is to be tried by external and internal evidence; the language and physical type of our race afford certain data for trying it, and other data are afforded by our literature, genius, and spiritual production generally. Data of this second kind belong to the province of the literary critic; data of this first kind to the province of the philologist and the physiologist.
>
> The province of the philologist and the physiologist is not mine; but this whole question as to the mixture of Celt with Saxon in us has been so little explored, people have been so prone to settle it off-hand according to their prepossessions, that even on the philological and physiological side of it I must say a few words in passing.[30]

---

[29] Ibid., p. 8.   [30] Ibid., pp. 66–67.

The ensuing discussion of what Arnold calls "physiology" is not what we should expect: it turns out that he is simply going to discuss the likelihood of mixture—that is, breeding—between the races. He cites, for example, the opinion of a certain Monsieur Edwards that "an Englishman who now thinks himself sprung from the Saxons or the Normans, is often in reality the descendant of the Britons."[31] The appeal to philology, on the other hand, might seem to suggest an alternative mechanism for the transmission of racial traits—namely, through language—but, in fact, philology is, for Arnold and his contemporaries, largely a guide to racial filiation, with those whose languages are most closely related being also most closely related by blood. Arnold is clear that language can, in fact, be misleading: "How little the triumph of the conqueror's laws, manners, and language, proves the extinction of the old race, we may see by looking at France; Gaul was Latinised in language manners, and laws, and yet her people remained essentially Celtic."[32] But he is also convinced, as I say, that it can be a guide to racial character.

Racialism

What Arnold lays out in these passages is the essence of what I call *racialism*. He believed—and in this he was typical of educated people in the English-speaking world of his day—that we could divide human beings into a small number of groups, called "races," in such a way that the members of these groups shared certain fundamental, heritable, physical, moral, intellectual, and cultural characteristics with one another that they did not share with members of any other race.

There are a few complications to this basic picture, which we should bear in mind. First, there are two major ways in which counterexamples to claims about the members of the race could simply be ruled out. It was acknowledged that there were, to

[31] Ibid., p. 72. Arnold never explicitly discusses sex, of course; and so we are left with the possibility of interpreting this as meaning either that there are Englishmen who are of wholly British (i.e., Celtic) descent or that there are some of partially British descent. Given, however, that some of the former have "passed" many centuries ago, the existence of the latter can be assumed.

[32] Ibid., p. 69.

begin with, in all races, as there are in animal species, occasional defective members: in animals, the two-headed pigs and three-legged cats so beloved of tabloid journalism in my homeland of Ghana: in human beings, the mute, the mentally disabled, the blind. These individuals were not to count against the general laws governing the racial type. Similarly, the norm for each race might be different for males and females, so that a racial type might be defined by two norms, rather than one.

A second complication derives from the fact that many of the characteristics of the various races were described as dispositions or tendencies: a single person who was not defective might still differ from the average member of his race because his individual character dominated the natural tendencies he had inherited in his racial essence. Celts might all tend toward the sentimental; but a particular Welshman might, through an exercise of will, conquer his natural racial temper. As a result, the failure of an individual to fit the norm for her race would not by itself refute the theory: for it might be that that person had simply conquered her inherited disposition. Many of what I shall call the characteristics of a race were thus not, to use a modern term, phenotypic: they did not necessarily display themselves in the observable behavior of every individual.[33]

These characteristics, then, that each normal woman (and man) of a race was supposed to share with every other woman (and man) together determined what we can call the *essence* of that race; they were characteristics that were necessary and sufficient, taken together, for someone to be a normal member of the race. Arnold's concept of race should, then, provide the materials for what I have called a strict criterial theory of the meaning of the term "race."

Arnold was uncharacteristic of his age in many ways: and one of them is the cosmopolitanism—or, at least, the Europeanism—of his temperament: he quotes frequently from French and German scholars. And on the question of race his views conformed with

[33] Nevertheless, it is a point about the logic of dispositional terms that it is hard (though not impossible) to make sense of applying them to the members of a group if no one in the group ever displays the disposition: see Anthony Appiah, *Assertion and Conditionals* (Cambridge: Cambridge University Press, 1985), chap. 2, sec. 4.

what was coming to be the common sense of Western European intellectuals.

Arnold's discussion in *On the Study of Celtic Literature* makes it plain that he believes that the racial essence accounts for more than the obvious visible characteristics of individuals and of groups—skin color, hair, shape of face—on the basis of which we decide whether people are, say, Asian- or Afro-Americans. For a racialist, then, to say someone is "Negro" is not just to say that she has inherited a black skin or curly hair: it is to say that her skin color goes along with other important inherited characteristics—including moral and literary endowments. By the end of the nineteenth century most Western scientists (indeed, most educated Westerners) believed that racialism was correct, and theorists sought to explain many characteristics—including, as we see here, the character of literatures—by supposing that they were inherited along with (or were in fact part of) a person's racial essence.

Mixing Essences

In the British people, Arnold is arguing, not only are there some whose ancestors are Celt—the first Britons—and some whose ancestors are Saxon, but these two lines have become literally joined through intermarriage, and the character of British literature is thus not only the product of a cultural syncretism but a joining of the essences of two races. Thus while the Celtic essence survives, it survives mixed with a Saxon essence: the character of the English thus contains both essences, both are available as driving energies of English poetry.

> All tendencies of human nature are in themselves vital and profitable; when they are blamed, they are to be blamed relatively, not absolutely. This holds true of the Saxon's phlegm as well as the Celt's sentiment. Out of the steady humdrum habit of the creeping Saxon, as the Celt calls him,—out of his way of going near the ground—has come, no doubt, Philistinism, that plane of essentially Germanic growth, flourishing with its genuine marks only in the German fatherland, Great Britain and her colonies, and the United States of America; but what a soul of goodness there is in Philistinism itself! and this soul of goodness I, who am often supposed

to be Philistinism's mortal enemy merely because I do not wish it to have things all its own way, cherish as much as anybody. This steady-going habit leads at last . . . up to science, up to the comprehension and interpretation of the world.[34]

Arnold has to account as well for the presence of Norman blood in this brew of racial essences, and once this is done he has all the elements he needs for constructing a picture of the British racial hybrid.

I have got a rough, but, I hope, clear notion of these three forces, the Germanic genius, the Celtic genius, the Norman genius. The Germanic genius has steadiness as its main basis, with commonness and humdrum for its defect, fidelity to nature for its excellence. The Celtic genius, sentiment as its main basis, with love of beauty, charm, and spirituality for its excellence, ineffectualness and self-will for its defect. The Norman genius, talent for affairs as its main basis, with strenuousness and clear rapidity for its excellence, hardness and insolence for its defect. And now to try and trace these in the composite English genius.[35]

Part of the evidence that Arnold offers that the character of England is the product of the intermixing of these racial types is in the contrast between English prose—exemplified in the news pages of the *London Times*—and German—exemplified in the *Cologne Gazett*. "At noon a long line of carriages extended from Pall Mall to the Peer's entrance of the Palace of Westminster," writes the correspondent of the *Times* (we must turn to the editorial pages to discover why it was known as "the Thunderer"). While the *Gazett* has: "Nachdem die Vorbereitungen zu dem auf dem Gürzenich-Saale zu Ehren der Abgeordneten Statt finden sollenden Bankette bereits vollständig getroffen worden waren, fand heute vormittag auf polizeiliche Anordnung die Schliessung sämmtlicher Zugänge zum Gürzenich Statt."[36] Arnold concludes: "Surely the mental habit of people who express their thoughts in so very different a manner, the one rapid, the other slow, the one plain, the other embarrassed, the one trailing, the other striding,

[34] Arnold, *On the Study of Celtic Literature*, pp. 83–84.
[35] Ibid., p. 87.   [36] Ibid., p. 88.

cannot be essentially the same."[37] It follows that there must be something other than the common Teutonic racial stock, which Germans and Saxons share, that accounts for the difference: this is evidence, then, on the racialist view, for the proposition that the British stock has been hybridized with some other race.

Arnold makes the same sort of appeal to race—this time at a greater level of generality, discussing the contrast between Indo-European and Semitic races—in *Culture and Anarchy*, a work that is much more widely known. In these essays, based on articles that first appeared in *Cornhill Magazine* in 1867 and 1868, and then in book form in 1869, Arnold wrote:

> Science has now made visible to everybody the great and pregnant elements of difference which lie in race, and in how signal a manner they make the genius and history of an Indo-European people vary from those of a Semitic people. Hellenism is of Indo-European growth, Hebraism of Semitic growth; and we English, a nation of Indo-European stock, seem to belong naturally to the movement of Hellenism. But nothing more strongly marks the essential unity of man than the affinities we can perceive, in this point or that, between members of one family of peoples and members of another; and no affinity of this kind is more strongly marked than that likeness in the strength and prominence of the moral fibre, which, notwithstanding immense elements of difference, knits in some special sort the genius and history of us English, and of our American descendants across the Atlantic, to the genius and history of the Hebrew people. Puritanism, which has been so great a power in the English nation, and in the strongest part of the English nation, was originally the reaction, in the seventeenth century, of the conscience and moral sense of our race, against the moral indifference and lax rule of conduct which in the sixteenth century came in with the Renascence. It was a reaction of Hebraism against Hellenism.[38]

Arnold makes a move here that is similar to the one he makes in the discussion of Celts and Saxons: he invokes race—which in Jefferson is invoked to account for division—in a context where he

[37] Ibid., pp. 88–89.
[38] Matthew Arnold, *Culture and Anarchy*, ed. Samuel Lipman (New Haven: Yale University Press, 1994), p. 95.

is arguing toward universality. Hebraism is Arnold's name for the tendencies in Western culture that are owed to what *we* would call its Judeo-Christian religious heritage: Arnold is convinced of the importance of Christianity and insists, in *Culture and Anarchy*, on the necessity of maintaining an established—that is, a state-supported—church in England. He is not, then, an enemy of Hebraism as such: every race, he insists here as much as in *On The Study of Celtic Literature*, has emblematic excellences as well as distinctive defects. The ideal for Britain, Arnold argues, is to construct a judicious mixture of Hebraism and Hellenism: the British, lacking Semitic blood, are not, by nature, Hebraists. The point, then, is that by Arnold's day even someone wanting to point to what was shared between two human groups was likely to do so in terms of the notion of race, a notion that was largely defined in terms of what separates people.[39]

These passages from the two sources, taken together, reveal a great deal of the structure of racialist thinking. Arnold displays both the flexibility of the view and some of its characteristic obscurities. Part of the flexibility flows from the fact that racial classification proceeds, as we see, at different levels: the Saxons and the Celts are both Indo-European. Differences between them are differences within the broader Indo-European race. When we need similarities, we can appeal to the higher level—the subsuming category of the Indo-European; when we need differences we can move lower down the taxonomic tree. In the United States, the differences between the Irish and the Anglo-Saxons could be used to account for the cultural and moral deficiencies—real or imaginary—of Irish immigrants; but their whiteness could be used to distinguish them from the Negro.

But there is also something of a muddle here: if the Celtic and the Saxon essences are so opposite, what is an individual like who inherits both of them? What would a man be like who was steady *and* sentimental; suffered from commonness and humdrummery

[39] Arnold's fairly benign mobilization of the idea of a Celtic race here contrasts favorably with contemporary and later uses of it in discussions of the Irish character both in England and in the United States. In late nineteenth-century America, the place of the Irish "race" within the broader European races was distinctly below that of the Anglo-Saxon and Nordic "races" and, in some contexts, closer to that of the Negro.

and ineffectualness and self-will; was faithful to nature and loved "beauty, charm, and spirituality"? What is lacking in Arnold's work is any theory of inheritance, any mechanism for explaining how the character of a race survives through the generations, transmitted in the bodies of its members: and any account of the laws that govern the interactions of racial essences. Without these, racialism makes no particular predictions about racial hybrids: a fact that is of the greatest importance since, if we are considering races at the taxonomic level of Celt and Saxon, there were very few peoples known to Arnold and his contemporaries who could plausibly have been thought to be unmixed.

What is also lacking is an answer to the question how we balance the effects of race and the effects of environment. *Culture and Anarchy* is in large measure about why the British are not Hellenic enough. If the British inherit naturally the tendencies of Hellenism with their Indo-European blood and language, why is British culture not too suffused with Hellenism (as the theory should predict) but too dominated by Hebraism? The answer Arnold gives has to do with the role of Christianity in spreading Hebraism, not by racial admixture but by cultural influence. And if the spread of Hebraism is a cultural phenomenon, then the Hellenism carried in the British blood, the racial essence, cannot be determinative of how a people will act. In *Celtic Literature* he says:

> And if,—whereas the Semitic genius placed its highest spiritual life in the religious sentiment, and made that the basis of its poetry,— the Indo-European genius places its highest spiritual life in the imaginative reason, and makes that the basis of its poetry, we are none the better for trying to make ourselves Semitic, when nature has made us Indo-European, and to shift the basis of our poetry. We may mean well; all manner of good may happen to us on the road we go; but we are not on our real right road, the road we must in the end follow.[40]

If this determinism of race is correct, isn't the Hebraism of England, described in *Culture and Anarchy*, evidence that the English are in fact not Indo-European but Semitic? And what signif-

---

[40] Arnold, *On the Study of Celtic Literature*, p. 113.

icance for the issue of environment versus racial essence should we give to the claim, in a letter of June 21, 1865, that "a nation is really civilised by acquiring the qualities it by nature is wanting in"?[41]

There is no doubt that these questions could have been answered: the idea, to which I referred earlier, that members of races inherited tendencies rather than more strictly phenotypic or behavioral properties could be invoked, for example, in an account of the interaction of racial character, individual traits, and environment. Indeed, in a period before Mendelism, it was possible to believe, with Lamarck, that the environment acted on individuals to produce in them changes that they transmitted to their children not through teaching but through bodily inheritance. After Mendel and Darwin, one can maintain that the environment acts on bodily heredity only slowly and over many generations;[42] but until then the distinction between cultural innovation, on the one hand, which allows a group to develop and transmit a new behavioral response extremely quickly, and biological change, which moves with a stately and glacial torpor, was unavailable. In Arnold's day, one could have argued that the Hebraism of England was both racially inherited and recently acquired: acquired, for example, in the first age of Puritanism.

Without answers to questions such as these, however, what is masquerading as an empirical, even a scientific, theory is remarkably insensitive to evidence. These deficiencies in Arnold are found in other race thinkers of the period—and, as we shall see, they are by no means limited to those who addressed the less physical—that is, the moral or cultural—traits of races.

The Origins of Literary Racialism

Arnold's identification of literature as a key to the national spirit is in a tradition we can trace back a century earlier to Johann Gottfried Herder.

[41] Joseph Carroll, *The Cultural Theory of Matthew Arnold* (Berkeley and Los Angeles: University of California Press, 1982).

[42] Perhaps one should also add August Weismann's doctrine of the separation of the somatoplasm and the germplasm as a crucial further bolster, from cytology, to this argument. See Garland Allen, *Life Science in the Twentieth Century*,

In his *On the New German Literature: Fragments* of 1767, Herder—who is, in some ways, the first important philosopher of modern nationalism—put forward the notion that language, far from being (as the received Aristotelian tradition had it) the merely material cause of a work of literature—that is, just what it happened to be written in—is not just "a tool of the arts and sciences" but "a part of them." "Whoever writes about the literature of a country," Herder continued, "must not neglect its language." Herder's notion of the *Sprachgeist*—literally the "spirit" of the language—embodies the thought that language is more than the medium through which speakers communicate.

Herder's ideas became part of mid-nineteenth-century common sense. The consensus was well expressed by Thomas Carlyle, the British essayist and man of letters, in 1831, less than a decade after Jefferson's *Autobiography*—in a discussion, in the *Edinburgh Review*, of a history of German poetry: "The History of a nation's poetry is the essence of its History, political, scientific, religious. With all these the complete Historian of a national poetry will be familiar: the national physiognomy, in its finest traits, and through its successive stages of growth, will be clear to him; he will discern the grand spiritual Tendency of each period."[43] That the "nation" here is not a political unit but a group defined by descent is evident from the fact that there was, in 1831, no single German state: Bismarck's time had not yet come. Between Carlyle's essay and Arnold's lectures, talk of "nations" was displaced by talk of "race."

Herder himself had had to make a sharp distinction between nations and states because in eighteenth-century Europe there was not even an approximate correlation between linguistic and political boundaries.[44] The modern European nationalism, which produced, for example, the German and Italian states, involved trying to create states to correspond to nationalities: nationalities conceived of as sharing a civilization and, more particularly, a lan-

---

Cambridge History of Science Series (Cambridge: Cambridge University Press, 1978).

[43] Thomas Carlyle, *Critical and Miscellaneous Essays: Collected and Republished*, vol. 3 (London: Chapman and Hall, 1869), p. 225.

[44] It is important to remember that the correlation remains in most parts of the world quite rough and ready.

guage and literature. Exactly because political geography did not correspond to Herder's nationalities, he was obliged to draw a distinction between the nation as a natural entity and the state as the product of culture, as a human artifice.

But with the increasing influence of the natural sciences—the separation out of specialties for natural history, and the increasing professionalization of scientific research—what is natural in human beings—the human nature whose story natural history told—came increasingly to be thought of as the province of such sciences as biology and anthropology. Inevitably, then, the nation comes more and more to be identified not just by common descent but also as a biological unit, defined by the shared essence that flows from that common descent.

Imposing the Herderian identification of the core of the nation with its national literature on top of the racial conception of the nation, we arrive at the racial understanding of literature that Arnold expresses: a way of thinking that flourishes from the mid–nineteenth century in the work of the first modern literary historians. Hippolyte Taine's monumental *History of English Literature*, published in France in the 1860s and perhaps the first modern literary history of English—begins with the words "History has been transformed, within a hundred years in Germany, within sixty in France, and that by the study of their literatures."[45] But he is soon telling us that "a race, like the Old Aryans, scattered from the Ganges as far as the Hebrides, settled in every clime, and every stage of civilization, transformed by thirty centuries of revolutions, nevertheless manifests in its languages, religions, literatures, philosophies, the community of blood and of intellect which to this day binds its offshoots together."[46] What is revealed, in short, by the study of literature that has transformed the discipline of history is the "moral state" of the race whose literature it is. It is because of this conception that Taine finds it proper to start his study of English literature with a chapter on the Saxons; so that chapter 1, book 1, of Taine's *History* begins not in England at all but in Holland: "As you coast the North Sea from Scheldt to Jutland, you will mark in the first place that the charac-

---

[45] Hippolyte A. Taine, *History of English Literature*, trans. H. Van Laun (London: Chatto and Windus, 1897), p. 1.

[46] Ibid., p. 17.

teristic feature is the want of slope: marsh, waster, shoal; the rivers hardly drag themselves along, swollen and sluggish, with long, black-looking waves."[47] The "Saxons, Angles, Jutes, Frisians . . . [and] Danes"[48] who occupied this region of Holland at the beginning of the first millennium are, according to Taine, the ancestors of the English; but since they, themselves, are of German descent, Taine also refers, in describing this "race" a few pages later, to some of the traits ascribed to Germans in Tacitus.

It is the conception of the binding core of the English nation as the Anglo-Saxon race that accounts for Taine's decision to identify the origins of English literature not in its antecedents in the Greek and Roman classics that provided the models and themes of so much of the best-known works of English "poesy"; not in the Italian models that influenced the drama of Marlowe and Shakespeare; but in *Beowulf*, a poem in the Anglo-Saxon tongue, a poem that was unknown to Chaucer and Spenser and Shakespeare, the first poets to write in a version of the English language that we can still almost understand.

Darwin and the Rise of Race Science

Arnold represents, then, a version of an older theory couched in terms of the new vocabulary of "race," whose authority derives, in part, from its association with the increasing prestige of the natural sciences. (You will have noticed that in the excerpts from the *Celtic Literature* lectures Arnold uses the word "data" several times.) And the most important theoretical development in the growth of a biological conception of race had already occurred by the time Arnold published *Culture and Anarchy* in 1869. For on November 24, 1859, Charles Darwin had published a work whose full title reads: *The Origin of Species by Means of Natural Selection or the Preservation of Favoured Races in the Struggle for Life.*

The word "race" had been used in this way to refer to kinds of animals and plants, as well as to kinds of people, for some time; but there is no doubt that even for a mid-nineteenth-century ear this title promises something of relevance to the study of human

[47] Ibid., p. 37.   [48] Ibid., p. 39.

difference. Indeed, the very fact that a single scientific theory promised to account for the variety of kinds of animals, in general, made its application to humans a natural step in the continuing process of placing the study of human anatomy in the context of a comparative zoology.

Darwin suggested, with characteristic caution, in *The Origin of Species*, that his theory might throw light on "the origin of man and his history"; the implication being that human beings developed, like other modern organisms, out of earlier forms. Taken to its "logical conclusion" this view suggested the oneness not only of all human beings—related by common descent—but, at least potentially, the common ancestry and thus unity of all life.

Darwin's theory can be thought of as consisting of two components: one is the claim that kinds of organisms develop by "descent with modification."[49] This claim was immediately widely accepted and applied to understanding the classification of organisms, representing, as it did, a continuation of arguments made five decades earlier by Lamarck.

But Darwin's more distinctive claim was that the mechanism of modification was natural selection: the selective survival of characteristics that gave individuals advantages in the "struggle for life." Darwin here drew on the parallelism with artificial selection of animals that was carried on by horse and cattle breeders and by pigeon fanciers. Just as they worked only with the natural variation among animals, selecting those with characteristics they favored and breeding from them, so, in Darwin's theory, nature "selected" organisms for breeding, not (as the rather colorful talk of the "struggle for life" suggested) by destroying some and allowing others to survive but by affecting differentially rates of reproductive success.

This claim was not so easily accepted. To begin with, it was not clear that there was sufficient variation within most kinds of organisms on which selection could work; and, indeed, though Darwin and Darwinians did stress the variability of natural populations, they had no account of the origin of the variations on which selection could act. More than this, most selective forces did not look as though they applied sufficient selection pressure

---

[49] My account here is based on Coleman, *Biology in the Nineteenth Century*.

65

to lead to any very substantial effects: it was only much later, with the development of population genetics, that it was possible to show that relatively small differences in survival rates could produce cumulatively large effects.

And, finally, Darwin had an inadequate and undeveloped theory of inheritance: the modern account, in terms of the gene, had no real impact until after Mendel's work was rediscovered in 1900. The theory of evolution by natural selection required that organisms should inherit the characteristics of their ancestors: otherwise the surviving offspring of an organism with a trait that gave it an advantage in the struggle for life offered no guarantee that its children would carry the same trait. Indeed, since Darwin believed in a sort of blending theory of inheritance, in which what accounted for a particular observable characteristic was the blended mixture of the factors that determined that characteristic in one's parents, he could not really explain why a factor that was rare in a population could survive at all, since it would be constantly "diluted" by more common forms.

There were other problems: if you want to treat all creatures as derived from a single ancient population, there must be some source of new variations: otherwise every characteristic in any modern organism must have existed in the earliest population. (Darwin was aware of "sports," creatures like the two-headed pigs to which I have already referred; but he thought—rightly, as it turns out—that these were of little importance in evolution.)

It is thus only with the development of Mendelism, with its account of inheritance in terms of genes and its recognition of the possibility of new variety arising by mutation, that the theory of natural selection was placed on a sound footing.

This second part of Darwin's theory—the view of natural selection—was thus rightly greeted with less immediate enthusiasm than the general idea of descent with modification.

Descent with modification was all that was required, however, to allow biology to give a much more straightforward account of how organisms should be classified. Darwin thought of species as essentially classificatory conveniences;[50] he was interested in how

---

[50] See George W. Stocking, *Race, Culture, and Evolution* (New York: Free Press, 1968), p. 46: "Darwin's own position on the question of human races was

populations changed their character and separated from each other, not in drawing boundaries between them. But his theory allowed that the accumulation of differences by selection could gradually produce kinds—varieties or species—that were measurably different; and thus suggested a mode of classification in which kinds that were more closely related by evolution should be classified together.

Thus the general acceptance of descent with modification and the increasing acceptance of Darwin's theory of natural selection gave scientific support to the idea that human kinds—races— could, like animal and plant species, be both evolutionarily related and biologically distinct. Furthermore, even though human races were not mutually infertile, the theory of evolution suggested a way of thinking of varieties as being in the process of speciation: races might not be species, but they were, so to speak, moving in that direction.

The Problem for a Biology of Race

Darwin, as I have said, thought of the species as essentially a classificatory convenience: he was, in philosophical jargon, a nominalist about species, holding that the boundaries between species were not clearly marked "in nature"; and if species were not marked in nature then varieties or subspecies (which is what, on his view, human races were), being even less distinct from one another than species, were presumably classificatory conveniences also.

To believe this was already to move away from the sort of racial essences that we find in Arnold. For Arnold, the interest of the characteristics of a race was exactly that you could suppose that its members all shared certain properties; so that having identified a person's race membership from her appearance one could then make inferences about her moral or literary dispositions. It makes sense that Darwin, whose whole analysis depends on the recogni-

---

equally congenial to polygenist thinking. Although he thought it a matter of indifference whether human races were called species or subspecies, he granted that a naturalist confronted for the first time with specimens of Negro and European man would doubtless call them 'good and true species.'"

tion of variation within populations, was more interested in the ways individuals differed from each other within their varieties than in the ways they were similar.

Once we have the modern genetic picture we can see that each person is the product of enormous numbers of genetic characteristics, interacting with one another and with an environment, and that there is nothing in the theory of evolution to guarantee that a group that shares one characteristic will share all or even most others. Characteristics on different chromosomes are, as the Mendelians said, independently assorted. The theory of evolution will also predict that as you move through a geographical range along a gradient of selection pressure, the frequency of certain characteristics—those that affect skin color, for example—may change fairly continuously, so that populations may blend into one another; and characteristics may drift from one neighboring population into another over time by intermarriage (or, to speak less euphemistically, interbreeding). Indeed, it turns out that, in humans, however you define the major races, the biological variability within them is almost as great as the biological variation within the species as a whole: put another way, while there are some characteristics that we are very good at recognizing—skin color, hair, skull shape—that are very unevenly geographically distributed, the groups produced by these assignments do not cluster much for other characteristics.

This fact was noticed by Ralph Waldo Emerson, only a few years after Arnold's essays. In 1876, in *his* essays on English traits, he wrote:

> An ingenious anatomist has written a book[51] to prove that races are imperishable, but nations are pliant constructions, easily changed or destroyed. But this writer did not found his assumed races on any necessary law, disclosing their ideal or metaphysical necessity; nor did he on the other hand count with precision the existing races and settle the true bounds; a point of nicety, and the popular test of his theory. The individuals at the extremes of divergence in one race of men are as unlike as the wolf to the lapdog. Yet each variety shades down imperceptibly into the next, and you cannot draw the line where a race begins or ends. Hence every writer

[51] The reference is to Robert Knox's *The Races of Men* (1850).

makes a different count. Blumenbach reckons five races; Humboldt three; and Mr. Pickering, who lately in our Exploring Expedition thinks he saw all kinds of men that can be on the planet, makes eleven.[52]

Even limiting oneself to the range of morphological criteria available to these comparative anatomists it is hard to classify people objectively into a small set of populations; and whichever way you do it, it will turn out that, for biological purposes, your classification will contain almost as much human genetic variation as there is in the whole species.[53]

"Race," then, as a biological concept, picks out, at best, among humans, classes of people who share certain easily observable physical characteristics, most notably skin color and a few visible features of the face and head.

The materials for an evolutionary explanation for skin color variation are easily laid out. The original human population had dark skins, which give you a selective advantage in the tropics, because they protect you somewhat from skin cancer. Lighter skins developed in colder climes, no doubt in part because skin cancer is less of a problem where you are permanently clothed, because of the cold, and the sun's rays pass more obliquely through the atmosphere. There may have been actual selection for white skins—maybe a landscape of mist and snow makes it easier to hide from your enemies—or it may just be that the mutations that make for white skin developed and survived because there was no longer selection pressure against them.[54] This sec-

[52] Ralph Waldo Emerson, *English Traits* (1876), vol. 5, Concord ed. (Boston: Houghton Mifflin, 1904), pp. 44–45.

[53] "On average there's .2 percent difference in genetic material between any two randomly chosen people on Earth. Of that diversity, 85 percent will be found within any local group of people—say, between you and your neighbor. More than half (9 percent) of the remaining 15 percent will be represented by differences between ethnic and linguistic groups within a given race (for example, between Italians and French). Only 6 percent represents differences between races (for example, between Europeans and Asians). And remember that's 6 percent of .2 percent. In other words, race accounts for only a minuscule .012 percent difference in our genetic material." Paul Hoffman, "The Science of Race," *Discover*, November 1994, p. 4.

[54] See Bernard R. Ortiz de Montellano, "Melanin, Afrocentricity and Pseudoscience," *Yearbook of Physical Anthropology* 36 (1993): 33–57.

ond possibility illustrates a form of evolutionary change that is of some importance, namely the development of populations whose character is the result not of adaptation but of the presence, by chance, in an isolated environment of a particular nonrepresentative sample of the total gene pool. And we may as well mention a third possibility here, one that Darwin noticed as well, which is that skin color was maintained by sexual selection: because, for some reason or other, human beings of one sex or other (or both) developed a preference for mates with lighter skins.

Why does biological variation in skin color not correlate more with other characteristics? Partly because the other characteristics have been selected (as has, say, sickle-cell disease in parts of West Africa and the Eastern Mediterranean) under pressures not highly correlated with the presence of harmful amounts of sunlight. Perhaps, too, because there are mechanisms that have evolved to maintain the stability of the genotype, reflecting, among other things, the fact that certain combinations of genes are adaptive only when they are present together.[55] As a result, even after long periods—of the order of hundreds of thousands of years—of geographical separation, human populations do not drift apart significantly with respect to most of their biological properties. And finally, because there has been continuous exchange of genes between the major geographical areas of human settlement over the hundreds of thousands of years since the first humans set off out of Africa.

The United States bears witness to the continuing significance of this phenomenon. It is true that Americans still tend, overwhelmingly, to marry people of their own, as we say, "racial identity." But very large numbers (perhaps as many as two-thirds) of African-Americans have some European forebears; up to two-fifths may have American Indian "blood"; and at least 5 percent of white Americans are thought to have African roots. It is estimated that 20 to 30 percent of the genes of the average African-American come from European and American Indian ancestors.[56]

[55] Ernst Mayr, *Populations, Species, and Evolution* (Cambridge: Harvard University Press, 1970), p. 300.

[56] James Shreve, "Terms of Estrangement," *Discover*, November 1994, p. 58. All these claims should be interpreted bearing in mind the fact that a "recent study found that in the early 1970s, 34 percent of the people participating in a

The result is that even if the four roughly separated populations of the four continents from which the ancestors of most Americans came had each been much less genetically variable than was in fact the case, there would still be large numbers of people whose skin color predicted very few other biological properties.

Why There Are No Races

We have followed enough of the history of the race concept and said enough about current biological conceptions to answer, on both ideational and referential views, the question whether there are any races.

On the ideational view, the answer is easy. From Jefferson to Arnold, the idea of race has been used, in its application to humans, in such a way as to require that there be significant correlations between the biological and the moral, literary, or psychological characters of human beings; and that these be explained by the intrinsic nature (the "talents" and "faculties" in Jefferson; the "genius," in Arnold) of the members of the race.[57]

That has turned out not to be true; the recent fuss generated by *The Bell Curve* about the correlation of race and IQ in the United States notwithstanding. Even if you believed Murray and Herrnstein's estimates of the heritability of IQ within groups in the United States—and you shouldn't—they offer almost no evidence relevant to refuting the claim that the differences between American groups are entirely caused by the environment; say, in particular, by the ways that blacks are treated in a racist society.[58]

---

census survey in two consecutive years changed racial groups from one year to the next."

[57] That is, *not* produced by the fact that people who have certain physical appearances are treated in ways that produce differences.

[58] Since this point is elementary it is perhaps worth explaining. Heritability measures the ratio of variance in a characteristic in an environment that is due to genes to the total variance. The heritability of height in the United States, in India, and in the human population in general is large. There is, too, a significant difference in average height between Indians (in India) and Americans (in America). But this interpopulational difference is almost entirely due to differences in nutrition. High heritability is quite consistent with most of the difference between populations being environmental.

Herrnstein and Murray, authors of *The Bell Curve* (New York: Free Press,

Once you have the modern theory of inheritance, you can see why there is less correlation than everyone expected between skin color and things we care about: people are the product not of essences but of genes interacting with one another and with environments, and there is little systematic correlation between the genes that fix color and the like and the genes that shape courage or literary genius. So, to repeat, on the ideational view we can say that nothing in the world meets the criteria for being a Jeffersonian or an Arnoldian race.

The biological notion of race was meant to account only for a narrower range of characteristics, namely, the biological ones, by which I mean the ones important for biological theory. There are certainly many ways of classifying people for biological purposes: but there is no single way of doing so that is important for most biological purposes that corresponds, for example, to the majority populations of each continent or subcontinent. It follows that on an ideational view, there are no biological races, either: not, in this case, because nothing fits the loose criteria but because too many things do.[59]

On the referential view we are required to find something in the world that best explains the history of usage of the term. Two candidates suggest themselves for the biological uses of "race": one is the concept of a population that I have been using for a while now. It can be defined as "the community of potentially interbreeding individuals at a given locality."[60] There are interesting discussions in the literature in population genetics as to how one should think about where to draw the boundaries of such communities: sometimes there is geographic isolation, which makes interbreeding in the normal course of things much less likely. But the population concept is generally used in such a way that we speak sometimes of a population defined by one geo-

1994), are aware of this fact and so seek to offer some rather unconvincing arguments for the suspicion that interracial average differences are in fact significantly genetic in origin. For arguments that they are *not*, see chap. 6 of Thomas Sowell's *Race and Culture: A World View* (New York: Basic Books, 1994).

[59] This is essentially the point of Jared Diamond's essay "Race without Color," in *Discover*, November 1994, pp. 82–89.

[60] Mayr, *Populations, Species, and Evolution*, p. 82.

graphical region and also, at other times, of a wider population, defined by a wider range, of which the first population is a part; and at yet other times of populations that are overlapping.

I have no problem with people who want to use the word "race" in population genetics.[61] What Darwin was talking about—evolution, speciation, adaptation—can best be understood in terms of talk of populations. And the fact is that in many plants and animals there are, in fact, local populations that are reproductively isolated from one another, different in clustered and biologically interesting ways, and still capable of interbreeding if brought artificially together; and biologists both before and after Darwin could have called these "races." It's just that this doesn't happen in human beings. In this sense, there are biological races in some creatures, but not in us.

A more ecumenical proposal in this spirit would be to say that the word "race" refers to populations, more generally. The trouble is that, in this sense, while there are human populations that are and have been for some time relatively reproductively isolated, it is not at all plausible to claim that any social subgroup in the United States is such a population. In *this* sense, then, there are human races, because there are human populations, in the geneticists' sense, but no large social group in America is a race. (The Amish, on the other hand, might come out as a race on this view, because they are a relatively reproductively isolated local population.)

A second candidate for the biological referent would simply be groups defined by skin color, hair, and gross morphology, corresponding to the dominant pattern for these characteristics in the major subcontinental regions: Europe, Africa, East and South Asia, Australasia, the Americas, and perhaps the Pacific Islands. This grouping would encompass many human beings quite ade-

---

[61] I think, however, that this usage carries two risks: first, it gives an ill-deserved legitimacy to ideas that are mistaken, because those who listen in on these conversations may not be aware of the fact that the usage here does not correspond at all to the groups that have mostly been called races in Europe and America; second, because speaking this way, you can actually find yourself relying, illicitly, on those other modes of classification. Still, if you can avoid these two dangers, there's no problem.

quately and some not at all: but it is hard to see of what biological *interest* it would be, since we can study the skin and gross morphology separately, and there is, at any rate, a good deal of variation within all these areas, in skin, hair color, and the morphology of the skull. Certainly this referent would not provide us with a concept that was central to biological thinking about human beings. And once more, in the United States, large numbers of people would not fit into any of these categories, because they are the products of mixtures (sometimes long ago) between people who do roughly fit this pattern, even though the social distinctions we call "racial" in the United States do, by contrast, cover almost everybody. And so, if we used this biological notion, it would have very little established correlation with any characteristics currently thought to be important for moral or social life.

The bottom line is this: you can't get much of a race concept, ideationally speaking, from any of these traditions; you can get various possible candidates from the referential notion of meaning, but none of them will be much good for explaining social or psychological life, and none of them corresponds to the social groups we call "races" in America.

PART 2. SYNTHESIS: FOR RACIAL IDENTITIES

"Speaking of Civilizations"

In 1911, responding to what was already clear evidence that race was not doing well as a biological concept, W.E.B. Du Bois, the African-American sociologist, historian, and activist, wrote in *The Crisis*, the magazine of the NAACP, which he edited:

> The leading scientists of the world have come forward . . . and laid down in categorical terms a series of propositions[62] which may be summarized as follows:
>
> 1. (a) It is not legitimate to argue from differences in physical characteristics to differences in mental characteristics . . .

---

[62] This claim was prompted by G. Spiller, ed., *Papers in Inter-Racial Problems Communicated to the First Universal Races Congress Held at the University of London, July 26–29, 1911* (London: P. S. King and Son, 1911). Republished with an introduction by H. Aptheker (Secaucus, N.J.: Citadel Press, 1970).

2. The civilization of a . . . race at any particular moment of time
offers no index to its innate or inherited capacities . . .[63]

And he concluded: "So far at least as intellectual and moral aptitudes are concerned we ought to speak of civilizations where we
now speak of races."[64] I have argued before that Du Bois's proposal to "speak of civilizations" turns out not to replace a biological notion but simply to hide it from view.[65] I think there are
various difficulties with the way that argument proceeded, and I
should like to do better. So let me try to reconstruct a sociohistorical view that has more merit than I have previously conceded.

Among the most moving of Du Bois's statements of the meaning of "race" conceived in sociohistorical terms is the one in *Dusk
of Dawn*, the "autobiography of a race concept," as he called it,
which he published in 1940. Du Bois wrote:

> The actual ties of heritage between the individuals of this group,
> vary with the ancestors that they have in common with many oth-
> ers: Europeans and Semites, perhaps Mongolians, certainly Ameri-
> can Indians. But the physical bond is least and the badge of color
> relatively unimportant save as a badge; the real essence of this kin-
> ship is its social heritage of slavery; the discrimination and insult;
> and this heritage binds together not simply the children of Africa,
> but extends through yellow Asia and into the South Seas. It is this
> unity that draws me to Africa.[66]

For reasons I shall be able to make clear only when I have given
my account, Du Bois's own approach is somewhat misleading. So

[63] W.E.B. Du Bois, "Races," in *Writings in Periodicals Edited by W.E.B.
Du Bois, Vol. 1, 1911–1925*, compiled and edited by Herbert Aptheker (Milwood, N.Y.: Kraus-Thomson Organization Limited, 1983), p. 13.

[64] Ibid., p. 14.

[65] "The Uncompleted Argument: Du Bois and the Illusion of Race," reprinted from *Critical Inquiry* 12 (Autumn 1985). In *"Race," Writing and Difference*, ed. Henry Louis Gates, Jr. (Chicago: University of Chicago Press,
1986), pp. 21–37. Lucius Outlaw has remonstrated with me about this in the
past; these rethinkings are prompted largely by discussion with him.

[66] Du Bois, *Dusk of Dawn: An Essay toward an Autobiography of a Race Concept* (New York: Harcourt, Brace, 1940). Reprinted with introduction by Herbert Aptheker (Milwood, N.Y.: Kraus-Thomson Organization Limited, 1975),
pp. 116–17.

instead of proceeding with exegesis of Du Bois, I must turn next to the task of shaping a sociohistorical account of racial identity. Still, as it turns out, it is helpful to start from Du Bois's idea of the "badge of color."

Racial Identity and Racial Identification[67]

I have argued that Jefferson and Arnold thought that when they applied a racial label they were identifying people with a shared essence. I have argued, also, that they were wrong—and, I insist, not slightly but wildly wrong. Earlier in American history the label "African" was applied to many of those who would later be thought of as Negroes, by people who may have been under the impression that Africans had more in common culturally, socially, intellectually, and religiously than they actually did. Neither of these kinds of errors, however, stopped the labeling from having its effects. As slavery in North America became racialized in the colonial period, being identified as an African, or, later, as a Negro, carrying the "badge of color," had those predictable negative consequences, which Du Bois so memorably captured in the phrase "the social heritage of slavery; the discrimination and insult."

If we follow the badge of color from "African" to "Negro" to "colored race" to "black" to "Afro-American" to "African-American" (and this ignores such fascinating detours as the route by way of "Afro-Saxon") we are thus tracing the history not only of a signifier, a label, but also a history of its effects. At any time in this history there was, within the American colonies and the United States that succeeded them, a massive consensus, both among those labeled black and among those labeled white, as to who, in their own communities, fell under which labels. (As immigration from China and other parts of the "Far East" occurred, an Oriental label came to have equal stability.) There was, no doubt, some "passing"; but the very concept of passing implies that, if the relevant fact about the ancestry of these individuals

---

[67] I am conscious here of having been pushed to rethink my views by Stuart Hall's Du Bois lectures at Harvard in the spring of 1994, which began with a nuanced critique of my earlier work on Du Bois's views.

had become known, most people would have taken them to be traveling under the wrong badge.

The major North American exception was in southern Louisiana, where a different system in which an intermediary Creole group, neither white nor black, had social recognition; but *Plessy v. Fergusson* reflected the extent to which the Louisiana Purchase effectively brought even that state gradually into the American mainstream of racial classification. For in that case Homer Adolph Plessy—a Creole gentleman who could certainly have passed in most places for white—discovered in 1896, after a long process of appeal, that the Supreme Court of the United States proposed to treat him as a Negro and therefore recognize the State of Louisiana's right to keep him and his white fellow citizens "separate but equal."

The result is that there are at least three sociocultural objects in America—blacks, whites and Orientals—whose membership at any time is relatively, and increasingly, determinate. These objects are historical in this sense: to identify all the members of these American races over time, you cannot seek a single criterion that applies equally always; you can find the starting point for the race—the subcontinental source of the population of individuals that defines its initial membership—and then apply at each historical moment the criteria of intertemporal continuity that apply at that moment to decide which individuals in the next generation count as belonging to the group. There is from the very beginning until the present, at the heart of the system, a simple rule that very few would dispute even today: where both parents are of a single race, the child is of the same race as the parents.

The criteria applicable at any time may leave vague boundaries. They certainly change, as the varying decisions about what proportion of African ancestry made one black or the current uncertainty as to how to assign the children of white-yellow "miscegenation" demonstrate. But they always definitely assign some people to the group and definitely rule out others; and for most of America's history the class of people about whom there was uncertainty (are the Florida Seminoles black or Indian?) was relatively small.[68]

[68] See Kevin Mulroy, *Freedom on the Border: The Seminole Maroons in Flor-*

Once the racial label is applied to people, ideas about what it refers to, ideas that may be much less consensual than the application of the label, come to have their social effects. But they have not only social effects but psychological ones as well; and they shape the ways people conceive of themselves and their projects. In particular, the labels can operate to shape what I want to call "identification": the process through which an individual intentionally shapes her projects—including her plans for her own life and her conception of the good—by reference to available labels, available identities.

Identification is central to what Ian Hacking has called "making up people."[69] Drawing on a number of examples, but centrally homosexuality and multiple personality syndrome, he defends what he calls a "dynamic nominalism," which argues that "numerous kinds of human beings and human acts come into being hand in hand with our invention of the categories labeling them."[70] I have just articulated a dynamic nominalism about a kind of person that is currently usually called "African-American."

Hacking reminds us of the philosophical truism, whose most influential formulation is in Elizabeth Anscombe's work on intention, that in intentional action people act "under descriptions"; that their actions are conceptually shaped. It follows, of course, that what people can do depends on what concepts they have available to them; and among the concepts that may shape one's action is the concept of a certain kind of person and the behavior appropriate to that kind.

Hacking offers as an example Sartre's brilliant evocation, in *Being and Nothingness*, of the Parisian *garçon de café*: "His movement is quick and forward, a little too precise, a little too rapid. He comes toward the patrons with a step a little too quick. He

---

ida, the Indian Territory, Coahuila, and Texas (Lubbock, Tex.: Texas Tech University Press, 1993).

[69] Ian Hacking, "Making Up People" reprinted from *Reconstructing Individualism: Autonomy, Individuality and the Self in Western Thought*, ed. Thomas Heller, Morton Sousa, and David Wellbery (Stanford: Stanford University Press, 1986), in *Forms of Desire: Sexual Orientation and the Social Constructionist Controversy*, ed. Edward Stein (New York: Routledge, 1992), pp. 69–88 (page references are to this version).

[70] Hacking, "Making Up People," p. 87.

bends forward a little too eagerly, his eyes express an interest too solicitous for the order of the customer."[71] Hacking comments:

> Sartre's antihero chose to be a waiter. Evidently that was not a possible choice in other places, other times. There are servile people in most societies, and servants in many, but a waiter is something specific, and a *garçon de café* more specific. . . .
>
> As with almost every way in which it is possible to be a person, it is possible to be a *garçon de café* only at a certain time, in a certain place, in a certain social setting. The feudal serf putting food on my lady's table can no more choose to be a *garçon de café* than he can choose to be lord of the manor. But the impossibility is evidently of a different kind.[72]

The idea of the *garçon de café* lacks, so far as I can see, the sort of theoretical commitments that are trailed by the idea of the black and the white, the homosexual and the heterosexual. So it makes no sense to ask of someone who has a job as a *garçon de café* whether that is what he really is. The point is not that we do not have expectations of the *garçon de café*: that is why it is a recognizable identity. It is rather that those expectations are about the performance of the role; they depend on our assumption of intentional conformity to those expectations. As I spent some time arguing earlier, we *can* ask whether someone is really of a black race, because the constitution of this identity is generally theoretically committed: we expect people of a certain race to behave a certain way not simply because they are conforming to the script for that identity, performing that role, but because they have certain antecedent properties that are consequences of the label's properly applying to them. It is because ascription of racial identities—the process of applying the label to people, including ourselves—is based on more than intentional identification that there can be a gap between what a person ascriptively is and the racial identity he performs: it is this gap that makes passing possible.

Race is, in this way, like all the major forms of identification that are central to contemporary identity politics: female and male; gay, lesbian, and straight; black, white, yellow, red, and brown; Jewish-, Italian-, Japanese-, and Korean-American; even

---

[71] Cited in ibid., p. 81.   [72] Ibid., p. 82.

that most neglected of American identities, class. There is, in all of them, a set of theoretically committed criteria for ascription, not all of which are held by everybody, and which may not be consistent with one another even in the ascriptions of a single person; and there is then a process of identification in which the label shapes the intentional acts of (some of) those who fall under it.

It does not follow from the fact that identification shapes action, shapes life plans, that the identification itself must be thought of as voluntary. I don't recall ever choosing to identify as a male;[73] but being male has shaped many of my plans and actions. In fact, where my ascriptive identity is one on which almost all my fellow citizens agree, I am likely to have little sense of choice about whether the identity is mine; though I *can* choose how central my identification with it will be—choose, that is, how much I will organize my life around that identity. Thus if I am among those (like the unhappily labeled "straight-acting gay men," or most American Jews) who are able, if they choose, to escape ascription, I may choose not to take up a gay or a Jewish identity; though this will require concealing facts about myself or my ancestry from others.

If, on the other hand, I fall into the class of those for whom the consensus on ascription is not clear—as among contemporary so-called biracials, or bisexuals, or those many white Americans of multiple identifiable ethnic heritages[74]—I may have a sense of identity options: but one way I may exercise them is by marking myself ethnically (as when someone chooses to wear an Irish pin) so that others will then be more likely to ascribe that identity to me.

Differences among Differences

Collective identities differ, of course, in lots of ways; the body is central to race, gender, and sexuality but not so central to class and ethnicity. And, to repeat an important point, racial identification is simply harder to resist than ethnic identification. The reason is twofold. First, racial ascription is more socially salient:

[73] That I don't recall it doesn't *prove* that I didn't, of course.
[74] See Mary C. Waters, *Ethnic Options: Choosing Identities in America* (Berkeley and Los Angeles: University of California Press, 1990).

unless you are morphologically atypical for your racial group, strangers, friends, officials are always aware of it in public and private contexts, always notice it, almost never let it slip from view. Second—and again both in intimate settings and in public space—race is taken by so many more people to be the basis for treating people differentially. (In this respect, Jewish identity in America strikes me as being a long way along a line toward African-American identity: there are ways of speaking and acting and looking—and it matters very little whether they are "really" mostly cultural or mostly genetic—that are associated with being Jewish; and there are many people, white and black, Jewish and Gentile, for whom this identity is a central force in shaping their responses to others.)

This much about identification said, we can see that Du Bois's analytical problem was, in effect, that he believed that for racial labeling of this sort to have the obvious real effects that it did have—among them, crucially, his own identification with other black people and with Africa—there must be some real essence that held the race together. Our account of the history of the label reveals that this is a mistake: once we focus, as Du Bois almost saw, on the racial badge—the signifier rather than the signified, the word rather than the concept—we see both that the effects of the labeling are powerful and real and that false ideas, muddle and mistake and mischief, played a central role in determining both how the label was applied and to what purposes.

This, I believe, is why Du Bois so often found himself reduced, in his attempts to define race, to occult forces: if you look for a shared essence you won't get anything, so you'll come to believe you've missed it, because it is super-subtle, difficult to experience or identify: in short, mysterious. But if, as I say, you understand the sociohistorical process of construction of the race, you'll see that the label works despite the absence of an essence.

Perhaps, then, we can allow that what Du Bois was after was the idea of racial identity, which I shall roughly define as a label, R, associated with *ascriptions* by most people (where ascription involves descriptive criteria for applying the label); and *identifications* by those that fall under it (where identification implies a shaping role for the label in the intentional acts of the possessors, so that they sometimes act *as an R*), where there is a history of associating possessors of the label with an inherited racial essence (even if some who use the label no longer believe in racial essences).

In fact, we might argue that racial identities could persist even if nobody believed in racial essences, provided both ascription and identification continue.

There will be some who will object to my account that it does not give racism a central place in defining racial identity: it is obvious, I think, from the history I have explored, that racism has been central to the development of race theory. In that sense racism has been part of the story all along. But you might give an account of racial identity in which you counted nothing as a racial essence unless it implied a hierarchy among the races;[75] or unless the label played a role in racist practices. I have some sympathy with the former strategy; it would fit easily into my basic picture. To the latter strategy, however, I make the philosopher's objection that it confuses logical and causal priority: I have no doubt that racial theories grew up, in part, as rationalizations for mistreating blacks, Jews, Chinese, and various others. But I think it is useful to reserve the concept of racism, as opposed to ethnocentrism or simply inhumanity, for practices in which a race concept plays a central role. And I doubt you can explain racism without first explaining the race concept.

I *am* in sympathy, however, with an animating impulse behind such proposals, which is to make sure that here in America we do not have discussions of race in which racism disappears from view. As I pointed out, racial identification is hard to resist in part because racial ascription by others is so insistent; and its effects—especially, but by no means exclusively, the racist ones—are so hard to escape. It is obvious, I think, that the persistence of racism means that racial ascriptions have negative consequences for some and positive consequences for others—creating, in particular, the white-skin privilege that it is so easy for people who have it to forget; and it is clear, too, that for those who suffer from the negative consequences, racial identification is a predictable response,

---

[75] This is the proposal of a paper on metaphysical racism by Berel Lang at the New School for Social Research seminar "Race and Philosophy" in October 1994, from which I learned much.

especially where the project it suggests is that the victims of racism should join together to resist it. I shall return later to some of the important moral consequences of present racism and the legacy of racisms of the past.

But before I do, I want to offer some grounds for preferring the account of racial identity I have proposed, which places racial essences at his heart, over some newer accounts that see racial identity as a species of cultural identity.

Cultural Identity in an Age of Multiculturalism

Most contemporary racial identification—whether it occurs in such obviously regressive forms as the white nationalism of the Aryan Nation or in an Afrocentrism about which, I believe, a more nuanced position is appropriate—most naturally expresses itself in forms that adhere to modified (and sometimes unreconstructed) versions of the old racial essences. But the legacy of the Holocaust and the old racist biology has led many to be wary of racial essences and to replace them with cultural essences. Before I turn to my final cautionary words about racial identifications, I want to explore, for a moment, the substitution of cultures for races that has occurred in the movement for multiculturalism.

In my dictionary I find as a definition for "culture" "the totality of socially transmitted behavior patterns, arts, beliefs, institutions, and all other products of human work and thought."[76] Like most dictionary definitions, this is, no doubt, a proposal on which one could improve. But it surely picks out a familiar constellation of ideas. That is, in fact, the sense in which anthropologists largely use the term nowadays. The culture of the Asante or the Zuni, for the anthropologist, includes every object they make—material culture—and everything they think and do.

The dictionary definition could have stopped there, leaving out the talk of "socially transmitted behavior patterns, arts, beliefs, institutions" because these *are* all products of human work and thought. They are mentioned because they are the residue of an older idea of culture than the anthropological one; something

---

[76] *American Heritage Dictionary III for DOS* (3d ed.) (Novato, Calif.: Wordstar International Incorporated, 1993).

more like the idea we might now express with the word "civilization": the "socially transmitted behavior patterns" of ritual, etiquette, religion, games, arts; the values that they engender and reflect; and the institutions—family, school, church, state—that shape and are shaped by them.[77] The habit of shaking hands at meetings belongs to culture in the anthropologist's sense; the works of Sandro Botticelli and Martin Buber and Count Basie belong to culture also, but they belong to civilization as well.

There are tensions between the concepts of culture and of civilization. There is nothing, for example, that requires that an American culture should be a totality in any stronger sense than being the sum of all the things we make and do.

American civilization, on the other hand, would have to have a certain coherence. Some of what is done in America by Americans would not belong to American civilization because it was too individual (the particular bedtime rituals of a particular American family); some would not belong because it was not properly American, because (like a Hindi sentence, spoken in America) it does not properly cohere with the rest.

The second, connected, difference between culture and civilization is that the latter takes values to be more central to the enterprise, in two ways. First, civilization is centrally defined by moral and aesthetic values: and the coherence of a civilization is, primarily, the coherence of those values with each other and, then, of the group's behavior and institutions with its values. Second, civilizations are essentially to be evaluated: they can be better and worse, richer and poorer, more and less interesting. Anthropologists, on the whole, tend now to avoid the relative evaluation of cultures, adopting a sort of cultural relativism, whose coherence philosophers have tended to doubt. And they do not take values as more central to culture than, for example, beliefs, ideas, and practices.

---

[77] The distinction between culture and civilization I am marking is not one that would have been thus marked in nineteenth-century ethnography or (as we would now say) social anthropology: culture and civilization were basically synonyms, and they were both primarily used in the singular. The distinctions I am making draw on what I take to be the contemporary resonances of these two words. If I had more time, I would explore the history of the culture concept the sort of way we have explored "race."

The move from "civilization" to "culture" was the result of arguments. The move away from evaluation came first, once people recognized that much evaluation of other cultures by the Europeans and Americans who invented anthropology had been both ignorant and biased. Earlier criticisms of "lower" peoples turned out to involve crucial misunderstandings of their ideas; and it eventually seemed clear enough, too, that nothing more than differences of upbringing underlay the distaste of some Westerners for unfamiliar habits. It is a poor move from recognizing certain evaluations as mistaken to giving up evaluation altogether, and anthropologists who adopt cultural relativism often preach more than practice it. Still, this cultural relativism was a response to real errors. That it is the wrong response doesn't make the errors any less erroneous.

The arguments against "civilization" were in place well before the midcentury. More recently, anthropologists began to see that the idea of the coherence of a civilization got in the way of understanding important facts about other societies (and, in the end, about our own). For even in some of the "simplest" societies, there are different values and practices and beliefs and interests associated with different social groups (for example, women as opposed to men). To think of a civilization as coherent was to miss the fact that these different values and beliefs were not merely different but actually opposed. Worse, what had been presented as the coherent unified worldview of a tribal people often turned out, on later inspection, to be merely the ideology of a dominant group or interest.

But the very idea of a coherent structure of beliefs and values and practices depends on a model of culture that does not fit our times—as we can see if we explore, for a moment, the ideal type of a culture where it might seem to be appropriate.

A Common Culture

There is an ideal—and thus to a certain extent imaginary—type of small-scale, technologically uncomplicated, face-to-face society, where most interactions are with people whom you know, that we call "traditional." In such a society every adult who is not mentally disabled speaks the same language. All share a vocabulary and a grammar and an accent. While there will be some words in the language that are not known by everybody—the names of medicinal herbs, the language of some religious rituals—most are known to all normal adults. To share a language is to participate in a complex set of mutual expectations and understandings: but in such a society it is not only linguistic behavior that is coordinated through universally known expectations and understandings. People will share an understanding of many practices—marriages, funerals, other rites of passage—and will largely share their views about the general workings not only of the social but also of the natural world. Even those who are skeptical about particular elements of belief will nevertheless know what everyone is supposed to believe, and they will know it in enough detail to behave very often as if they believed it, too.

A similar point applies to many of the values of such societies. It may well be that some people, even some groups, do not share the values that are enunciated in public and taught to children. But, once more, the standard values are universally known, and even those who do not share them know what it would be to act in conformity with them and probably do so much of the time.

In such a traditional society we may speak of these shared beliefs, values, signs, and symbols as the common culture; not, to insist on a crucial point, in the sense that everyone in the group actually holds the beliefs and values but in the sense that everybody knows what they are and everybody knows that they are widely held in the society.

Now, the citizens of one of those large "imagined communities" of modernity we call "nations" need not have, in this sense, a common culture. There is no single shared body of ideas and practices in India, or, to take another example, in most contemporary African states. And there is not now and there has never been a common culture in the United States, either. The reason is simple: the United States has always been multilingual, and has always had minorities who did not speak or understand English. It has always had a plurality of religious traditions; beginning with American Indian religions and Puritans and Catholics and Jews and including now many varieties of Islam, Buddhism, Jainism, Taoism, Bahai, and so on. And many of these religious traditions have been quite unknown to one another. More than this, Americans have also always differed significantly even among those who do speak English, from North to South and East to West, and from country to city, in customs of greeting, notions of civility, and a whole host of other ways. The notion that what has held the United States together historically over its great geographical range is a common culture, like the common culture of my traditional society, is—to put it politely—not sociologically plausible.

The observation that there is no common American national culture will come as a surprise to many: observations about American culture, taken as a whole, are common. It is, for example, held to be individualist, litigious, racially obsessed. I think each of these claims is actually true, because what I mean when I say there is no common culture of the United States is not what is denied by someone who says that there is an American culture.

Such a person is describing large-scale tendencies within American life that are not necessarily participated in by all Americans. I do not mean to deny that these exist. But for such a tendency to be part of what I am calling the *common culture* they would have to derive from beliefs and values and practices (almost) universally shared and known to be so. And *that* they are not.

At the same time, it has also always been true that there was a dominant culture in these United States. It was Christian, it spoke English, and it identified with the high cultural traditions of Europe and, more particularly, of England. This dominant culture included much of the common culture of the dominant classes— the government and business and cultural elites—but it was familiar to many others who were subordinate to them. And it was not merely an effect but also an instrument of their domination.

The United States of America, then, has always been a society of many common cultures, which I will call, for convenience, subcultures, (noting, for the record, that this is not the way the word is used in sociology).

It would be natural, in the current climate, with its talk of multiculturalism, to assume that the primary subgroups to which these subcultures are attached will be ethnic and racial groups (with religious denominations conceived of as a species of ethnic group). It would be natural, too, to think that the characteristic

87

difficulties of a multicultural society arise largely from the cultural differences between ethnic groups. I think this easy assimilation of ethnic and racial subgroups to subcultures is to be resisted.

First of all, it needs to be argued, and not simply assumed, that black Americans, say, taken as a group, *have* a common culture: values and beliefs and practices that they share and that they do not share with others. This is equally true for, say, Chinese-Americans; and it is a fortiori true of white Americans. What seems clear enough is that being an African-American or an Asian-American or white is an important social identity in the United States. Whether these are important social identities because these groups have shared common cultures is, on the other hand, quite doubtful, not least because it is doubtful whether they *have* common cultures at all.

The issue is important because an analysis of America's struggle with difference as a struggle among cultures suggests a mistaken analysis of how the problems of diversity arise. With differing cultures, we might expect misunderstandings arising out of ignorance of each others' values, practices, and beliefs; we might even expect conflicts because of differing values or beliefs. The paradigms of difficulty in a society of many cultures are misunderstandings of a word or a gesture; conflicts over who should take custody of the children after a divorce; whether to go to the doctor or to the priest for healing.

Once we move from talking of cultures to identities whole new kinds of problems come into view. Racial and ethnic identities are, for example, essentially contrastive and relate centrally to social and political power; in this way they are like genders and sexualities.

Now, it is crucial to understanding gender and sexuality that women and men and gay and straight people grow up together in families, communities, denominations. Insofar as a common culture means common beliefs, values, and practices, gay people and straight people in most places have a common culture: and while there are societies in which the socialization of children is so structured by gender that women and men have seriously distinct cultures, this is not a feature of most "modern" societies. And it is perfectly possible for a black and a white American to grow up together in a shared adoptive family—with the same knowledge and values—and still grow into separate racial identities, in part because their experience outside the family, in public space, is bound to be racially differentiated.

I have insisted that we should distinguish between cultures and identities; but ethnic identities characteristically have cultural distinctions as one of their primary marks. That is why it is so easy to conflate them. Ethnic identities are created in family and community life. These—along with mass-mediated culture, the school, and the college—are, for most of us, the central sites of the social transmission of culture. Distinct practices, ideas, norms go with each ethnicity in part because people *want* to be ethnically distinct: because many people want the sense of solidarity that comes from being unlike others. With ethnicity in modern society, it is often the distinct identity that comes first, and the cultural distinction that is created and maintained because of it—not the other way around. The distinctive common cultures of ethnic and religious identities matter not simply because of their contents but also as markers of those identities.

In the United States, not only ethnic but also racial boundaries are culturally marked. In *White Women, Race Matters: The Social Construction of Whiteness*,[78] Ruth Frankenberg records the anxiety of many white women who do not see themselves as white "ethnics" and worry, therefore, that they have no culture.[79] This is somewhat puzzling in people who live, as every normal human being does, in rich structures of knowledge, experience, value and meaning; through tastes and practices: it is perplexing, in short, in people with normal human lives. But the reason these women do not recognize that they have a culture is because none of these things that actually make up their cultural lives are marked as white, as belonging specially to them: and the things that *are* marked as white (racism, white privilege) are things they want to repudiate. Many African-Americans, on the other hand, have cultural lives in which the ways they eat, the churches they go to, the

[78] Ruth Frankenberg, *White Women, Race Matters: The Social Construction of Whiteness* (Minneapolis: University of Minnesota Press, 1993).
[79] The discussion of this work is shaped by conversation with Larry Blum, Martha Minow, David Wilkins, and David Wong.

music they listen to, and the ways they speak *are* marked as black: their identities are marked by cultural differences.

I have insisted that African-Americans do not have a single culture, in the sense of shared language, values, practices, and meanings. But many people who think of races as groups defined by shared cultures, conceive that sharing in a different way. They understand black people as sharing black culture *by definition*: jazz or hip-hop belongs to an African-American, whether she likes it or knows anything about it, because it is culturally marked as black. Jazz belongs to a black person who knows nothing about it more fully or naturally than it does to a white jazzman.

What Matters about Culture: Arnold Again

This view is an instance of what my friend Skip Gates has called "cultural geneticism."[80] It has, in Bertrand Russell's wicked phrase, "the virtues of theft over honest toil." On this view, you earn rights to culture that is marked with the mark of your race— or your nation—simply by having a racial identity. For the old racialists, as we saw, your racial character was something that came with your essence; this new view recognizes that race does not bring culture, and generously offers, by the wave of a wand, to correct Nature's omission. It is as generous to whites as it is to blacks. Because Homer and Shakespeare are products of Western culture, they are awarded to white children who have never studied a word of them, never heard their names. And in this generous spirit the fact is forgotten that cultural geneticism deprives white people of jazz and black people of Shakespeare. This is a bad deal—as Du Bois would have insisted. "I sit with Shakespeare," the Bard of Great Barrington wrote, "and he winces not."

There is nothing in cultural geneticism of the ambition or the rigor of Matthew Arnold's conception, where culture is, as he says in *Culture and Anarchy*, "the disinterested and active use of reading, reflection and observation,"[81] and what is most valuable to us

---

[80] Gates means the notion to cover thinking in terms of cultural patrimony quite generally, not just in the case of race. See Henry Louis Gates, Jr., *Loose Canons* (New York: Oxford University Press, 1993).

[81] Arnold, *Culture and Anarchy*, p. 119.

in culture, in the anthropological sense, is earned by intellectual labor, by self-cultivation. For Arnold, true culture is a process "which consists in becoming something rather than in having something, in an inward condition of the mind and spirit";[82] whose aim is a "perfection in which characters of beauty and intelligence are both present, which unites, 'the two noblest of things,'—as Swift, who of one of the two, at any rate, had himself all too little, most happily calls them in his *Battle of the Books*,— 'the two noblest of things, sweetness and light.' "[83]

Arnold's aim is not, in the proper sense, an elitist one: he believes that this cultivation is the proper aim of us all.

> This is the *social idea*; and the men of culture are the true apostles of equality. The great men of culture are those who have had a passion for diffusing, for making prevail, for carrying from one end of society to the other, the best knowledge, the best ideas of their time; who have laboured to divest knowledge of all that was harsh, uncouth, difficult, abstract, professional, exclusive; to humanise it, to make it efficient outside the clique of the cultivated and learned, yet still remaining the *best* knowledge and thought of the time, and a true source, therefore, of sweetness and light.[84]

If you have this view of culture, you will think of cultural geneticism as the doctrine of the ignorant or the lazy, or at least of those who pander to them. And it is a view of culture whose adoption would diminish any society that seriously adopted it.

Not only is the conflation of identities and cultures mistaken, the view of cultural possession that underlies that error is the view of the Philistine, who, in Arnold's translation of Epictetus, makes "a great fuss about exercise, a great fuss about eating, a great fuss about drinking, a great fuss about walking, a great fuss about riding. All these things ought to be done merely *by the way*: the formation of the spirit and character must be our real concern."[85]

---

[82] Ibid., p. 33.   [83] Ibid., p. 37.

[84] Ibid., p. 48. The phrase "sweetness and light" is from Jonathan Swift's *Battle of the Books* (1697). The contest between the ancients (represented there by the bee) and the moderns (represented by the spider) is won by the ancients, who provide, like the bee, both honey and wax—sweetness and light. Sweetness is, then, aesthetic, and light intellectual, perfection.

[85] Arnold, *Culture and Anarchy*, p. 36.

Identities and Norms

I have been exploring these questions about culture in order to show how unsatisfactory an account of the significance of race that mistakes identity for culture can be. But if this is the wrong route from identity to moral and political concerns, is there a better way?

We need to go back to the analysis of racial identities. While the theories on which ascription is based need not themselves be normative, these identities come with normative as well as descriptive expectations; about which, once more, there may be both inconsistency in the thinking of individuals and fairly widespread disagreement among them. There is, for example, a very wide range of opinions among American Jews as to what their being Jewish commits them to; and while most Gentiles probably don't think about the matter very much, people often make remarks that suggest they admire the way in which, as they believe, Jews have "stuck together," an admiration that seems to presuppose the moral idea that it is, if not morally obligatory, then at least morally desirable, for those who share identities to take responsibility for each other. (Similar comments have been made increasingly often about Korean-Americans.)

We need, in short, to be clear that the relation between identities and moral life are complex. In the liberal tradition, to which I adhere, we see public morality as engaging each of us as individuals with our individual "identities": and we have the notion, which comes (as Charles Taylor has rightly argued[86]) from the ethics of authenticity, that, other things being equal, people have the right to be acknowledged publicly as what they already really are. It is because someone is already authentically Jewish or gay that we deny them something in requiring them to hide this fact, to "pass," as we say, for something that they are not. Charles Taylor has suggested that we call the political issues raised by this fact the politics of recognition: a politics that asks us to acknowledge socially and politically the authentic identities of others.

As has often been pointed out, however, the way much discus-

[86] Charles Taylor, *Multiculturalism and "The Politics of Recognition."* With commentary by Amy Gutmann, ed., K. Anthony Appiah, Jürgen Habermas, Steven C. Rockefeller, Michael Walzer, and Susan Wolf (Princeton: Princeton University Press, 1994).

sion of recognition proceeds is strangely at odds with the individualist thrust of talk of authenticity and identity. If what matters about me is my individual and authentic self, why is so much contemporary talk of identity about large categories—race, gender, ethnicity, nationality, sexuality—that seem so far from individual? What is the relation between this collective language and the individualist thrust of the modern notion of the self? How has social life come to be so bound up with an idea of identity that has deep roots in romanticism with its celebration of the individual over against society?[87]

The connection between individual identity, on the one hand, and race and other collective identities, on the other, seems to be something like this: each person's individual identity is seen as having two major dimensions. There is a collective dimension, the intersection of her collective identities; and there is what I will call a personal dimension, consisting of other socially or morally important features of the person—intelligence, charm, wit, cupidity—that are not themselves the basis of forms of collective identity.

The distinction between these two dimensions of identity is, so to speak, a sociological rather than a logical distinction. In each dimension we are talking about properties that are important for social life. But only the collective identities count as social categories, kinds of person. There is a logical category but no social category of the witty, or the clever, or the charming, or the greedy: people who share these properties do not constitute a social group, in the relevant sense. The concept of authenticity is central to the connection between these two dimensions; and there is a problem in many current understandings of that relationship, a misunderstanding one can find, for example, in Charles Taylor's recent (brilliant) essay *Multiculturalism and the Politics of Recognition*.

Authenticity

Taylor captures the ideal of authenticity in a few elegant sentences: "There is a certain way of being that is *my* way. I am called upon to live my life in this way. . . . If I am not [true to myself],

---

[87] Taylor reminds us rightly of Trilling's profound contributions to our understanding of this history. I discuss Trilling's work in chap. 4 of *In My Father's House*.

I miss the point of my life."[88] To elicit the problem, here, let me start with a point Taylor makes in passing about Herder: "I should note here that Herder applied his concept of originality at two levels, not only to the individual person among other persons, but also to the culture-bearing people among other peoples. Just like individuals, a Volk should be true to itself, that is, its own culture."[89] It seems to me that in this way of framing the issue less attention than necessary is paid to the connection between the originality of persons and of nations. After all, in many places nowadays, the individual identity, whose authenticity screams out for recognition, is likely to have an ethnic identity (which Herder would have seen as a national identity) as a component of its collective dimension. It is, among other things, my being, say, an African-American that shapes the authentic self that I seek to express.[90] And it is, in part, because I seek to express my self that I seek recognition of an African-American identity. This is the fact that makes problems: for recognition as an African-American means social acknowledgment of that collective identity, which requires not just recognizing its existence but actually demonstrating respect for it. If, in understanding myself as African-American, I see myself as resisting white norms, mainstream American conventions, the racism (and, perhaps, the materialism or the individualism) of "white culture," why should I at the same time seek recognition from these white others?

There is, in other words, at least an irony in the way in which an ideal—you will recognize it if I call it the bohemian ideal—in which authenticity requires us to reject much that is conventional in our society is turned around and made the basis of a "politics of recognition."

Irony is not the bohemian's only problem. It seems to me that this notion of authenticity has built into it a series of errors of philosophical anthropology. It is, first of all, wrong in failing to see what Taylor so clearly recognizes, namely the way in which the self is, as he says, dialogically constituted. The rhetoric of authenticity proposes not only that I have a way of being that is all

[88] Taylor, *Multiculturalism*, p. 30.
[89] Ibid., p. 31.
[90] And, for Herder, this would be a paradigmatic national identity.

my own but that in developing it I must fight against the family, organized religion, society, the school, the state—all the forces of convention. This is wrong, however, not only because it is in dialogue with other people's understandings of who I am that I develop a conception of my own identity (Charles Taylor's point) but also because my identity is crucially constituted through concepts (and practices) made available to me by religion, society, school, and state, and mediated to varying degrees by the family (Hacking's point about "making up people"). Dialogue shapes the identity I develop as I grow up: but the very material out of which I form it is provided, in part, by my society, by what Taylor calls its language in "a broad sense."[91] I shall borrow and extend Taylor's term "monological" here to describe views of authenticity that make these connected errors.

I used the example of African-Americans just now, and it might seem that this complaint cannot be lodged against an American black nationalism: African-American identity, it might be said, is shaped by African-American society, culture, and religion. "It is dialogue with these black others that shapes the black self; it is from these black contexts that the concepts through which African-Americans shape themselves are derived. The white society, the white culture, over against which an African-American nationalism of the counterconventional kind poses itself, is therefore not part of what shapes the collective dimension of the individual identities of black people in the United States."

This claim is simply wrong. And what shows it is wrong is the fact that it is in part a recognition of a black identity by "white society" that is demanded by nationalism of this form. And "recognition" here means what Taylor means by it, not mere acknowledgment of one's existence. African-American identity, as I have argued, is centrally shaped by American society and institutions: it cannot be seen as constructed solely within African-American communities. African-American culture, if this means shared beliefs, values, practices, does not exist: what exists are African-American cultures, and though these are created and sus-

---

[91] The broad sense "cover[s] not only the words we speak, but also other modes of expression whereby we define ourselves, including the 'languages' of art, of gesture, of love, and the like" (p. 32).

tained in large measure by African-Americans, they cannot be understood without reference to the bearers of other American racial identities.

There is, I think, another error in the standard framing of authenticity as an ideal, and that is the philosophical realism (which is nowadays usually called "essentialism") that seems inherent in the way questions of authenticity are normally posed. Authenticity speaks of the real self buried in there, the self one has to dig out and express. It is only later, after romanticism, that the idea develops that one's self is something that one creates, makes up, so that every life should be an artwork whose creator is, in some sense, his or her own greatest creation. (This is, I suppose, an idea one of whose sources is Oscar Wilde; but it is surely very close to the self-cultivation that Arnold called "culture.")

Of course, neither the picture in which there is just an authentic nugget of selfhood, the core that is distinctively me, waiting to be dug out, nor the notion that I can simply make up any self I choose, should tempt us. We make up selves from a tool kit of options made available by our culture and society—in ways that I pointed out earlier. We do make choices, but we don't determine the options among which we choose.[92]

If you agree with this, you will wonder how much of authenticity we should acknowledge in our political morality: and that will depend, I suppose, on whether an account of it can be developed that is neither essentialist nor monological.

It would be too large a claim that the identities that claim recognition in the multicultural chorus *must* be essentialist and monological. But it seems to me that one reasonable ground for suspicion of much contemporary multicultural talk is that the conceptions of collective identity they presuppose are indeed remarkably unsubtle in their understandings of the processes by which identities, both individual and collective, develop. The story I have told for African-American identity has a parallel for other collective identities: in all of them, I would argue, false theories play a central role in the application of the labels; in all of them the story is complex, involves "making up people," and cannot be explained by an appeal to an essence.

[92] This is too simple, too, for reasons captured in Anthony Giddens's many discussions of "duality of structure."

Beyond Identity

The large collective identities that call for recognition come with notions of how a proper person of that kind behaves: it is not that there is *one* way that blacks should behave, but that there are proper black modes of behavior. These notions provide loose norms or models, which play a role in shaping the life plans of those who make these collective identities central to their individual identities; of the identifications of those who fly under these banners.[93] Collective identities, in short, provide what we might call scripts: narratives that people can use in shaping their life plans and in telling their life stories. In our society (though not, perhaps, in the England of Addison and Steele) being witty does not in this way suggest the life script of "the wit." And that is why what I called the personal dimensions of identity work differently from the collective ones.

This is not just a point about modern Westerners: cross-culturally it matters to people that their lives have a certain narrative unity; they want to be able to tell a story of their lives that makes sense. The story—my story—should cohere in the way appropriate by the standards made available in my culture to a person of my identity. In telling that story, how I fit into the wider story of various collectivities is, for most of us, important. It is not just gender identities that give shape (through, for example, rites of passage into woman- or manhood) to one's life: ethnic and national identities too fit each individual story into a larger narrative. And some of the most "individualist" of individuals value such things. Hobbes spoke of the desire for glory as one of the dominating impulses of human beings, one that was bound to make trouble for social life. But glory can consist in fitting and being seen to fit into a collective history: and so, in the name of glory, one can end up doing the most social things of all.

How does this general idea apply to our current situation in the multicultural West? We live in societies in which certain individuals have not been treated with equal dignity because they were, for example, women, homosexuals, blacks, Catholics. Because,

---

[93] I say "make" here not because I think there is always conscious attention to the shaping of life plans or a substantial experience of choice but because I want to stress the antiessentialist point that there are choices that can be made.

as Taylor so persuasively argues, our identities are dialogically shaped, people who have these characteristics find them central—often, negatively central—to their identities. Nowadays there is a widespread agreement that the insults to their dignity and the limitations of their autonomy imposed in the name of these collective identities are seriously wrong. One form of healing of the self that those who have these identities participate in is learning to see these collective identities not as sources of limitation and insult but as a valuable part of what they centrally are. Because the ethics of authenticity requires us to express what we centrally are in our lives, they move next to the demand that they be recognized in social life as women, homosexuals, blacks, Catholics. Because there was no good reason to treat people of these sorts badly, and because the culture continues to provide degrading images of them nevertheless, they demand that we do cultural work to resist the stereotypes, to challenge the insults, to lift the restrictions.

These old restrictions suggested life scripts for the bearers of these identities, but they were negative ones. In order to construct a life with dignity, it seems natural to take the collective identity and construct positive life scripts instead.

An African-American after the Black Power movement takes the old script of self-hatred, the script in which he or she is a nigger, and works, in community with others, to construct a series of positive black life scripts. In these life scripts, being a Negro is recoded as being black: and this requires, among other things, refusing to assimilate to white norms of speech and behavior. And if one is to be black in a society that is racist then one has constantly to deal with assaults on one's dignity. In this context, insisting on the right to live a dignified life will not be enough. It will not even be enough to require that one be treated with equal dignity despite being black: for that will require a concession that being black counts naturally or to some degree against one's dignity. And so one will end up asking to be respected *as a black*.

I hope I seem sympathetic to this story. I *am* sympathetic. I see how the story goes. It may even be historically, strategically necessary for the story to go this way.[94] But I think we need to go on

<hr/>

[94] Compare what Sartre wrote in his "Orphée Noir," in *Anthologie de la Nou-*

to the next necessary step, which is to ask whether the identities constructed in this way are ones we can all be happy with in the longer run. What demanding respect for people *as blacks* or *as gays* requires is that there be some scripts that go with being an African-American or having same-sex desires. There will be proper ways of being black and gay: there will be expectations to be met; demands will be made. It is at this point that someone who takes autonomy seriously will want to ask whether we have not replaced one kind of tyranny with another. If I had to choose between Uncle Tom and Black Power, I would, of course, choose the latter. But I would like not to have to choose. I would like other options. The politics of recognition requires that one's skin color, one's sexual body, should be politically acknowledged in ways that make it hard for those who want to treat their skin and their sexual body as personal dimensions of the self. And "personal" doesn't mean "secret" but "not too tightly scripted," "not too constrained by the demands and expectations of others."

In short, so it seems to me, those who see potential for conflict between individual freedom and the politics of identity are right.

Why Differences between Groups Matter

But there is a different kind of worry about racial identities; one that has not to do with their being too tightly scripted but with a consequence of their very existence for social life. We can approach the problem by asking why differences between groups matter.

This is, I think, by no means obvious. If some minority groups—Korean-Americans, say—do especially well, most people feel, "More power to them." We worry, then, about the minorities that fail. And the main reason why people currently worry about minorities that fail is that group failure may be evidence of injustice to individuals. That is the respectable reason why there is so much interest in hypotheses, like those of Murray and Herrn-

---

velle Poésie Nègre et Malagache de Langue Francaise, ed. L. S. Senghor, p. xiv. Sartre argued, in effect, that this move is a necessary step in a dialectical progression. In this passage he explicitly argues that what he calls an "antiracist racism" is a path to the "final unity . . . the abolition of differences of race."

stein, that suggest a different diagnosis. But let us suppose that we can get rid of what we might call Sowellian discrimination: discrimination, that is, as understood by Thomas Sowell, which is differential treatment based on false (or perhaps merely unwarranted) beliefs about the different average capacities of racial groups.[95]

Even without Sowellian discrimination socioeconomic disparities between groups threaten the fairness of our social arrangements. This issue can be kept clear only if we look at the matter from the point of view of an individual. Suppose I live in a society with two groups, blacks and whites. Suppose that, for whatever reason, the black group to which I obviously belong scores averagely low on a test that is genuinely predictive of job performance. Suppose the test is expensive. And suppose I would have, in fact, a high score on this test and that I would, in fact, perform well.[96] In these circumstances it may well be economically rational for an employer, knowing what group I belong to, simply not to give me the test, and thus not to hire me.[97] The employer has acted in a rational fashion; there is no Sowellian discrimination here. But most people will understand me if I say that I feel that this outcome is unfair. One way of putting the unfairness is to say, "What I can do and be with my talents is being held back because others, over whose failings I have no control, happen to have the characteristics they do."

Capitalism—like life—is full of such unfairness: luck—from lot-

---

[95] "Once the possibility of economic performance differences between groups is admitted, then differences in income, occupational 'representation,' and the like do not, in themselves, imply that decision-makers took race or ethnicity into account. However, in other cases, group membership may in fact be used as a proxy for economically meaningful variables, rather than reflecting either mistaken prejudices or even subjective affinities and animosities." Thomas Sowell, *Race and Culture*, p. 114.

[96] You need both these conditions, because a high score on a test that correlates well for some skill doesn't necessarily mean you will perform well. And, in fact, Sowell discusses the fact that the same IQ score predicts different levels of economic success for different ethnic groups; ibid., pp. 173, 182.

[97] Knowing this, I might offer to pay myself, if I had the money: but that makes the job worth less to me than to members of the other groups. So I lose out again.

teries to hurricanes—affects profit. And we can't get rid of all unfairness; for if we had perfect insurance, zero risk, there'd be no
role for entrepreneurship, no markets, no capitalism. But we do
think it proper to mitigate some risks. We think, for example, that
we should do something about bad luck when it has large negative effects on individual people, or if it forces them below some
socioeconomic baseline—we insure for car accidents, death, loss
of home; the government helps those ruined by large-scale acts of
God. We don't worry much about the chance production of small
negative effects on individuals, even large numbers of individuals.

It is at least arguable that in our society the cost to competent,
well-behaved individual blacks and Hispanics[98] of being constantly treated as if they have to measure up—the cost in stress, in
anger, in lost opportunities—is pretty high.[99] It would be consistent with a general attitude of wanting to mitigate risks with large
negative consequences for individuals to try to do something
about it.[100]

This specific sort of unfairness—where a person is atypically
competent in a group that is averagely less competent—is the result, among other things, of the fact that jobs are allocated by a
profit-driven economy and the fact that I was born into a group
in which I am atypical. The latter fact may or may not be the consequence of policies adopted by this society. Let's suppose it isn't:
so society isn't, so to speak, causally responsible. According to
some—for example, Thomas Sowell, again—that means it isn't
morally responsible, either: you don't have to fix what you didn't
break.

I'm not so sure. First, we can take collective responsibility, "as
a society," for harms we didn't cause; as is recognized in the
Americans with Disabilities Act. But second, the labor market is,

---

[98] Let me explicitly point out that many of these people are not middle-class.

[99] I actually think that there is still rather more Sowellian discrimination than
Sowell generally acknowledges; but that is another matter.

[100] It will seem to some that I've avoided an obvious argument here, which is
that the inequalities in resources that result from differences in talents under
capitalism need addressing. I agree. But the argument I am making here is
meant to appeal to only extremely unradical individualist ideas; it's designed not
to rely on arguing for egalitarian outcomes directly.

after all, an institution: in a modern society it is kept in place by such arrangements as the laws of contract, the institution of money, laws creating and protecting private property, health and safety at work, and equal employment laws. Sowell may disapprove of some of these, but he can't disapprove of all of them; without all of them, there'd be no capitalism. So the outcome is the result not only of my bad luck but of its interaction with social arrangements, which could be different.

Thus once we grasp the unfairness of this situation, people might feel that something should be done about it. One possible thing would be to try to make sure there were no ethnic minorities significantly below norm in valuable skills. If the explanation for most significant differences between groups is not hereditary, this could be done, in part, by adopting policies that discouraged significant ethnic differentiation, which would gradually produce assimilation to a single cultural norm. Or it could be done by devoting resources most actively to the training of members of disadvantaged groups.

Another—more modest—move would be to pay special attention to finding talented members of minority groups who would not be found when employers were guided purely by profit.

A third—granted once more that the differences in question are not largely hereditary—would be to explore why there are such differences and to make known to people ways of giving themselves or their children whatever aptitudes will maximize their life chances, given their hereditary endowments.

Fourth, and finally, for those differences that were hereditary it would be possible to do research to seek to remedy the initial distribution by the genetic lottery—as we have done in making it possible for those without natural resistance to live in areas where malaria and yellow fever are endemic.

Each of these strategies would cost something, and the costs would be not only financial. Many people believe that the global homogenization of culture impoverishes the cultural fabric of our lives. It is a sentiment, indeed, we find in Arnold: "My brother Saxons have, as is well known, a terrible way with them of wanting to improve everything but themselves off the face of the earth; I have no passion for finding nothing but myself everywhere; I like variety to exist and to show itself to me, and I would not for the world have the lineaments of the Celtic genius lost."[101] The first strategy—of cultural assimilation—would undoubtedly escalate that process. And all these strategies would require more knowledge than we now have to apply in actual cases so as to guarantee their success. Anyone who shares my sense that there is an unfairness here to be met, an unfairness that has something to do with the idea that what matters is individual merit, should be interested in developing that kind of knowledge.

But I want to focus for a moment on a general effect of these four strategies. They would all produce a population less various in some of the respects that make a difference to major socioeconomic indicators. This would not mean that everybody would be the same as everybody else—but it could lead to a more recreational conception of racial identity. It would make African-American identity more like Irish-American identity is for most of those who care to keep the label. And that would allow us to resist one persistent feature of ethnoracial identities: that they risk becoming the obsessive focus, the be-all and end-all, of the lives of those who identify with them. They lead people to forget that their individual identities are complex and multifarious—that they have enthusiasms that do not flow from their race or ethnicity, interests and tastes that cross ethnoracial boundaries, that they have occupations or professions, are fans of clubs and groups. And they then lead them, in obliterating the identities they share with people outside their race or ethnicity, away from the possibility of identification with Others. Collective identities have a tendency, if I may coin a phrase, to "go imperial," dominating not only people of other identities, but the other identities, whose shape is exactly what makes each of us what we individually and distinctively are.

In policing this imperialism of identity—an imperialism as visible in racial identities as anywhere else—it is crucial to remember always that we are not simply black or white or yellow or brown, gay or straight or bisexual, Jewish, Christian, Moslem, Buddhist, or Confucian but that we are also brothers and sisters; parents and children; liberals, conservatives, and leftists; teachers and lawyers and auto-makers and gardeners; fans of the Padres and the Bruins;

---

[101] Arnold, *On the Study of Celtic Literature*, p. 11.

amateurs of grunge rock and lovers of Wagner; movie buffs; MTV-holics, mystery-readers; surfers and singers; poets and pet-lovers; students and teachers; friends and lovers. Racial identity can be the basis of resistance to racism; but even as we struggle against racism—and though we have made great progress, we have further still to go—let us not let our racial identities subject us to new tyrannies.

In Conclusion

Much of what I have had to say in this essay will, no doubt, seem negative. It is true that I have defended an analytical notion of racial identity, but I have gone to worry about too hearty an endorsement of racial identification. Let me quote Matthew Arnold again, for the last time: "I thought, and I still think, that in this [Celtic] controversy, as in other controversies, it is most desirable both to believe and to profess that the work of construction is the fruitful and important work, and that we are demolishing only to prepare for it."[102] So here are my positive proposals: live with fractured identities; engage in identity play; find solidarity, yes, but recognize contingency, and, above all, practice irony.[103] In short I have only the proposals of a banal "postmodernism." And there is a regular response to these ideas from those who speak for the identities that now demand recognition, identities toward which so many people have struggled in dealing with the obstacles created by sexism, racism, homophobia. "It's all very well for you. You academics live a privileged life; you have steady jobs; solid incomes; status from your place in maintaining cultural capital. Trifle with your own identities, if you like; but leave mine alone."

To which I answer only: my job as an intellectual is to call it as I see it. I owe my fellow citizens respect, certainly, but not a feigned acquiescence. I have a duty to reflect on the probable consequences of what I say; and then, if I still think it worth saying, to accept responsibility for them. If I am wrong, I say, you do not need to plead that I should tolerate error for the sake of

[102] Ibid., p. ix.

[103] See, for example, Richard Rorty, *Contingency, Irony and Solidarity* (New York: Cambridge University Press, 1989), and my review of it: "Metaphys. Ed.," *Village Voice*, September 19, 1989, p. 55.

human liberation; you need only correct me. But if I am right, so it seems to me, there is a work of the imagination that we need to begin.

And so I look forward to taking up, along with others, the fruitful imaginative work of constructing collective identities for a democratic nation in a world of democratic nations; work that must go hand in hand with cultivating democracy here and encouraging it everywhere else. About the identities that will be useful in this project, let me say only this: the identities we need will have to recognize *both* the centrality of difference within human identity *and* the fundamental moral unity of humanity.

Responding to Racial Injustice

✳

AMY GUTMANN

> In what public discourse does the reference to black
> people not exist? It exists in every one of this nation's
> mightiest struggles. . . . It is there in the construction
> of a free and public school system; the balancing of
> representation in legislative bodies; jurisprudence
> and legal definitions of justice.
> *(Toni Morrison)*

> "Mr. Ashe, I guess this must be the heaviest burden
> you have ever had to bear, isn't it?" she asked finally.
> I thought for a moment, but only a moment. "No,
> it isn't. It's a burden, all right. But AIDS isn't the
> heaviest burden I have had to bear."
> "Is there something worse? Your heart attack?"
> I didn't want to detain her, but I let the door close
> with both of us still inside. "You're not going to believe
> this," I said to her, "but being black is the greatest
> burden I've had to bear."
> "You can't mean that."
> ". . . I stand by my remark. Race is for me a more
> onerous burden than AIDS. My disease is the result of
> biological factors over which we, thus far, have had no
> control. Racism, however, is entirely made by people,
> and therefore it hurts and inconveniences infinitely
> more."
> *(Arthur Ashe)*

> My inheritance was particular, specifically limited and
> limiting: my birthright was vast, connecting me to all
> that lives, and to everyone, forever. But one cannot
> claim the birthright without accepting the inheritance.
> *(James Baldwin)*

RACIAL INJUSTICE may be the most morally and intellectually vexing problem in the public life of this country.[1] How should we respond? I doubt there is a simple or single way of responding. As a political philosopher and a citizen of the United States, I develop a political morality for a society still suffering from racial injustice. My response to racial injustice in the United States need not be yours, but I hope to convince you that all citizens should respond and try to justify our responses to one another rather than wish the problem would go away or be taken care of by others.

I focus in this essay on responding to racial injustice toward black Americans, but nothing I say should suggest that injustice toward black Americans is the only surviving, systematic instantiation of racial injustice in the United States. Nonetheless, the issue of racial injustice toward black Americans is certainly among the most long-standing, systematic, and vexing examples of racial injustice in our society. We should not be deterred from focusing on this urgent issue because there are other examples of racial injustice, or injustice with no racial source, also (urgently) to be addressed.

One of those issues is the economic injustice of this society. Economic injustice exacerbates racial injustice, and is often diffi-

Tali Mendelberg and David Wilkins provided invaluable comments on an early draft, as did Samuel Fleischacker and Dennis Thompson on a subsequent draft. Responses by Anthony Appiah, Daniel A. Bell, Jorge Garcia, Kent Greenawalt, Jeff Spinner-Halev, George Kateb, Elizabeth Kiss, Jacob Levy, Christine Korsgaard, Stephen Macedo, Michelle Moody-Adams, Joseph Schwartz, Harold Shapiro, Yael Tamir, and Stuart White led me to rethink some parts of my argument. I also benefited from a wide range of comments by participants in the Laurance S. Rockefeller Fellows' Seminar at the University Center for Human Values, the Rutgers University Conference "Race: Its Meaning and Significance," and the Patten Foundation Lectures at Indiana University. I am grateful to Susan Moller Okin and Michael Bratman for inviting me to give the Tanner Lectures at Stanford University, and to members of the Philosophy Department and the Ethics and Society Program at Stanford for their intellectual engagement and hospitality while I was their guest as a Tanner lecturer. I received able research assistance from Christianne Hardy, Kyle Hudson, Jacob Levy, and Jack Nowlin.

[1] By *racial* injustice I mean any injustice whose source includes either present or past discrimination based on race. By racial discrimination, I mean any morally indefensible distinctions based on race.

cult to distinguish from racial injustice because it disproportionately harms black Americans. But economic injustice injures poor people of every skin color. The lack of full employment, the absence of adequate welfare and child care, and the presence of grossly unfair income and wealth distributions are cause for grave concern quite apart from the problem of racial injustice, but these problems also exacerbate racial injustice, making it all the more difficult to overcome. Many political philosophers, myself included, have said a great deal about economic injustice while neglecting to consider the issue of racial injustice, and so I concentrate on racial injustice in this essay.[2]

In the course of developing general theories of justice, political philosophers have cogently claimed that a just society must secure for every individual a set of basic liberties and basic opportunities—those opportunities would include adequate education, health care, work, and basic income if work is unavailable or supplementary income if work does not adequately pay. I cannot overemphasize the importance of our striving to make good on this unfulfilled promise of a constitutional democracy with liberty and justice for all.

Yet racial injustice in this society today is not simply derivative of economic and educational injustice, however much it is exacerbated by injustices in these realms. Principles of economic and educational equity therefore are inadequate to resolve the problem of racial injustice. Were they adequate, the problem would be relatively simple to resolve by applying the same color blind morality that would be suitable in an ideal society to our nonideal one. But when we take a close look at the claims of an ideal color blind morality applied without modification to our nonideal society, we see much that is mistaken with such a simple application.

PART 1. WHY QUESTION THE TERMS OF OUR PUBLIC DEBATE?

In public debate about racial issues today, as in the past, many people claim that our society must be bound by the same morality that would be suitable to a just society. That morality, they say, is

---

[2] *Liberal Equality* (Cambridge: Cambridge University Press, 1980).

fundamentally color blind, and to diverge from color blindness is to make the mistake of thinking that two wrongs make a right. It is simply wrong, on this commonly articulated view, to address the injustice of racial preferences against blacks with the equal and opposite injustice of racial preferences against nonblacks. However obvious it may be that two wrongs do not make a right, it is far from obvious that diverging from color blindness is wrong in a society that is still suffering from racial injustice.

The claim on the part of morally motivated people that color blindness is the uniquely correct response to racial injustice is understandable, for principles of justice are typically conceived with the model of an ideal society in mind. Furthermore, most of us first learn about fairness in family contexts where color consciousness would be out of place, or taught for pernicious purposes. When we are taught to take principles of justice seriously, whether as children or as students and scholars, we learn those principles that have been developed for an ideal society. This does not constitute a wholesale critique either of our upbringing or of our philosophical traditions, but it does signal a serious, neglected limitation of our moral education of which we should be aware. It would be a blatant contradiction for a political philosophy to posit an ideal society that is beset by a legacy of racial injustice. The principles that most of us learn, from childhood to maturity, are therefore color blind not because color blindness is the right response to racial injustice but rather because color blindness is the ideal morality (for an ideal society).

But the color blind response to injustice in our society is doubly mistaken. Color blindness is not a fundamental principle of justice. Nor is it the strongest interpretation of such a principle for our society. Fairness is a fundamental principle of justice, and—as I explore in the second part of this essay—it is a principle that does not always call for color blindness, at least not with regard to employment, university admissions, or electoral redistricting in our nonideal society. To respond to racial injustice with a color conscious principle or policy is therefore not to commit any wrong at all, provided the principle or policy is consistent with fairness.

Fairness does not therefore call only or even primarily for color conscious policies. It calls first and foremost for economic and educational policies that provide every individual, regardless of skin color, with a full set of basic liberties and basic opportunities. Many of these educational and economic policies could be color blind. For example, a policy of providing productive work that pays for every adult who is able to work need not be, and probably should not be, a color conscious policy. Nonetheless, we probably cannot determine the kind of work that would be most productive in our society without being color conscious at least to the extent of recognizing the special needs of those who have suffered the effects of racial discrimination. The need for color blind policies as contrasted with color conscious policies is therefore not a simple matter, and not one that can be decided in the abstract. Abstract principles of justice are color blind. This is not surprising, since they are constructed by imagining what a just society would look like. The fair application of abstract principles, by contrast, may be color conscious. This should not surprise us either, because a fair application entails looking carefully at an actual society rather than imagining or assuming the ideal.

The United States is not only beset by economic and educational injustices that afflict the least advantaged regardless of their race. It is also beset by injustices that afflict individuals *because* of their skin color, various facial features, and assumed ancestry, along with the racial identity that is socially attached to these physical features and assumed ancestry. (I shall call the package of physical characteristics a person's "color," although it typically refers to more than skin color alone.) Because a child's life chances in the United States today vary with his or her color, even after controlling for other factors (such as parental income and education), fairness itself may call for color conscious policies, which would not be appropriate in a just society. Were we to close our minds to this possibility by invoking an absolute principle of color blindness, then we would also be cutting ourselves off from addressing the enduring legacy of racial discrimination that afflicts this democracy. We would be acting as if the legacy of racial injustice does not exist, or had been entirely overcome, or is morally irrelevant to public policy, or is not something with which we must be concerned either as democratic citizens or as moral beings.

Some defenders of color blindness recognize that color conscious policies may be defensible *in principle*, but they think that color conscious policies are invariably counterproductive and therefore criticize them as indefensible in practice. They argue that racial preferences should be replaced by class preferences for pragmatic reasons of coalition building rather than for principled reasons of fairness. The pursuit of "class, not race" policies has recently been called "the hottest idea in the affirmative action debate."[3] On closer examination, the idea turns out to be hot, but only half-baked. Class conscious policies are necessary to address economic injustice, but not sufficient to address racial injustice.

In the third part of this essay, I show why class conscious policies are not an adequate substitute for race conscious policies either in principle or in practice. Class conscious policies are urgently needed in this country. They should include programs that create enough jobs that pay a living wage, provide adequate child care for parents so they can afford to work, secure a real safety net for those who cannot work, and institute adequate educational programs for the children of poor parents. But until all the necessary class conscious policies are in place, a fair response to racial injustice still may include a wide range of color conscious policies. And even if all the necessary class conscious policies were in place, some color conscious policies might still be necessary before the United States could become a fully just society.

However much we might wish otherwise, class conscious *and* color conscious policies are both necessary, neither sufficient, to address racial injustice. Why, then, does such an acrimonious debate rage among Americans who support one or the other kind of policy if both kinds can be justified? Is it simply that most citizens are not morally motivated and therefore support what seems to be in our narrow interest, depending on our class or color? This debunking explanation is popular, especially among the press, but it is unsupported by the diverse responses to this controversy *within* groups that are identified by class or color. The range of responses to racial injustice among black Americans is no less than that among white Americans. The responses among middle-class Americans and every other large social group are similarly diverse.

[3] Michael Kinsley, "The Spoils of Victimhood," *New Yorker*, March 27, 1995, p. 66. Kinsley is a critic of the idea. One of the best of many defenses, which I discuss below, is Richard Kahlenberg, "Class, Not Race," *New Republic*, April 3, 1995, pp. 21–26.

We should expect the controversy to continue raging because it is not enough, morally speaking, to call for "class *and* color" instead of "class, not color" policies, even though "class *and* color" points in the more morally promising direction. Not all color conscious policies or all kinds of color consciousness are right. A simple sound bite answer on either side of this controversy will therefore not get us very far. No wonder the controversy continues to be so polarized and acrimonious.

In the fourth part of this essay, I try to show why two diametrically opposed responses to racial injustice in legislative representation—one that insists on color blindness and the other that aims at race proportional representation—are too simple. Until recent redistricting plans took effect in some states, such as North Carolina, black citizens had elected very few, if any, representatives of their choice to Congress since Reconstruction. One of the simplest defenses of redistricting in North Carolina would be to endorse race proportional representation in legislatures. Carve up the state so as to ensure that black North Carolinians, who constitute approximately 20 percent of the electorate, elect 20 percent of the legislators. If we assume that this is the aim of recent redistricting plans, then we are driven to expose the injustice and unconstitutionality of such an undemocratic aim. But if race proportionality is not the actual aim of redistricting, then this controversy calls for far more, and better, public deliberation than it has yet received.

As does another issue that underlies much of the debate over racial injustice, which the fifth section of this essay examines: the meaning and value of color consciousness. In considering the value of color consciousness, we would do well to distinguish it from race consciousness. Race consciousness assumes that racial identity is a scientifically based fact of differentiation among individuals that has morally relevant implications for public policy. Color consciousness rejects this idea of racial identity. But color consciousness recognizes the ways in which skin color and other superficial features of individuals adversely and unfairly affect their life chances. What's right about color consciousness, I hope to show by the end of this essay, is also the partial truth in color blindness: all human beings regardless of their color should be treated as free and equal beings, worthy of the same set of basic liberties and opportunities.

This basic moral insight is better captured by color consciousness than by color blindness. But color consciousness, unlike race consciousness, recognizes that race is a fiction that often functions *sotto voce* as scientific fact in the identification of individuals. The fiction is that something called "race"—typically identified by skin color and facial features, sometimes coupled with information about ancestry—sorts individual human beings into genetically distinguishable subgroups (or subspecies) that are properly identified as races and that can be meaningfully treated as such for both scientific and social purposes.[4] Proponents of both color blindness and color consciousness agree that the fiction of racial identification cannot survive scrutiny. It is therefore best brought out in the open among open-minded people. Similar skin color and other discernible physical features do not a race, or subspecies, make. Moreover, were there a scientific fact of different races among human beings, this in itself would not come close to justifying any of the discriminatory treatment that has constituted racial injustice in this country.

It is nonetheless important that we expose the fiction of race because it has, however illogically, served pernicious social purposes. People who use the term "race" to refer to human subgroupings often assume or imply the existence of a meaningful scientific referent that indicates something more than the presence of genes for mere morphological characteristics such as skin pigmentation or facial features. Yet scientists have not established the existence of human subspecies, or races; and few think the pursuit very promising. Quite the contrary, they have not found any scientifically meaningful way to sort people into separate groups on the basis of large packaged sets of genetic differences that are relatively stable over time. Although the existence of human subspecies would not justify any of the conventional forms

---

[4] "Today, when we use the term 'race,' we are actually talking about the social construction of differences." Darlene Clark Hine, "'In the Kingdom of Culture': Black Women and the Intersection of Race, Gender, and Class," in *Lure and Loathing: Essays on Race, Identity, and the Ambivalence of Assimilation*, ed. Gerald Early (New York: Penguin Books, 1994), p. 338.

of racial discrimination, our muddled thinking about race continues to contribute to the psychology of racial differentiation that perpetuates racial injustice.

Another common usage of race—which I shall call "color"—refers only to superficial features such as skin color and facial characteristics, and occasionally also to ancestry. Were this all that race meant today, then it would not be a morally dangerous fiction. Nor would race be a very significant social or scientific category, around which some of the most vexing political problems of our time revolve. Because the common usage of race often assumes and conveys much more than superficial morphological differences, it is important to distinguish race consciousness from color consciousness (even though the latter does not refer only to color, literally understood). In light of our legacy of racial discrimination, we ignore the distinction at the risk of perpetuating misunderstandings along with injustices.

Although I concentrate on the injustices in this essay (since they can survive exposure of the scientific fiction of race), I should say a bit more here about the misunderstandings that are often embedded in the common usage of race. The moral case for responding to racial injustice does not rest on disproving the idea that there are separate human races. Even if we knew that there were different races among human beings, this "fact" would not provide any reason to deny basic liberties and opportunities to any individual human beings by virtue of their racial identity. But, human psychology being what it is, the moral case against racial injustice is unlikely to be as effective if people continue to believe in the fiction of distinguishable human races.

As far as scientists now know, the superficial differences that often trigger common references to someone as a member of this or that race are not accompanied by a large set of biological differences that would meaningfully distinguish human beings as members of different subspecies for scientific purposes. Scientists have not found a large, relatively stable set of genetic similarities—beyond the morphological differences—among the people commonly categorized as black or white or any other race according to ordinary usage. Even the morphological differences are not as distinct as many people assume. One does not have to be a scien-

114

tist to know that "black" Americans have an enormously broad range of skin colors and facial features, as do "white" Americans. This should not surprise us, because black and white Americans have greatly mixed ancestries. Something similar may be said for the other groups in the United States that are categorized by the official Census as different races.

Scientists estimate that 20 to 30 percent of the genetic material of African-Americans derives from European or American Indian ancestors.[5] Facial features and skin color certainly vary among regions of the world, and among people whom Americans call black and white, but the variations in these features are not part of a large packaged set of genetic variations that would warrant the scientific separation of blacks and whites into two races.[6] Neither the traditional one drop of (black) blood rule for identifying someone as black nor the once official one-sixteenth black ancestry rule makes biological sense, but these were among the rules of recognition that defined and perpetuated the dominant understanding of race in the United States.[7]

Scientists calculate that the average genetic difference between two randomly chosen individuals is .2 percent (two *tenths* of one percent!) of the total genetic material. Of that genetic diversity, 85 percent can be found between neighbors. Nine of the remaining 15 percent can be found between ethnic or linguistic groups. Six percent represents differences among geographically more separate groups, such as Europeans and Asians. If Europeans and Asians are considered separate races, only .012 percent— .00012!—of their genetic differences is accounted for by their "race."[8] And those genetic differences that can be accounted for have little or no scientific, let alone moral, importance.

Today, black and white Americans are racially distinguished for political purposes not by a scientific standard or the one drop of blood rule but (ostensibly) by self-identification. In light of our

[5] James Shreeve, "Terms of Estrangement," *Discover*, November 1994, p. 58.
[6] Ibid.
[7] For a summary of these conventional rules and recent efforts to introduce new categories of race and ethnicity into public policy, see Lawrence Wright, "One Drop of Blood," *New Yorker*, July 25, 1994, pp. 46–55.
[8] See Paul Hoffman, "The Science of Race," *Discover*, November 1994, p. 4.

history, we should not infer from this practice of self-identification that racial identification is voluntary.[9] By the time the vast majority of Americans fill out the census forms, enrollment forms for schools, application forms for jobs, and governmental mortgage, scholarship, and loan forms asking what race we and our children are, we have been told the answer by the way we have been treated ever since we were too young to choose for ourselves. Our self-categorizations (currently into black, white, American Indian or Alaskan Native, Asian or Pacific Islander) are neither voluntaristic nor scientific.[10] "These sorts of distinctions," as Anthony Appiah puts it, "are not—as those who believe in races apparently suppose—markers of deeper biologically based racial essences, correlating closely with most (or even many) important biological (let alone nonbiological) properties."[11]

What scientists do know about genetic similarities and differences among large groups of people therefore suggests that everyday distinctions do not remotely correspond to a scientific understanding of race.[12] Although scientists have recently made great strides in locating specific genes for various diseases, there is no

[9] The results of a recent study, however, find that "in the early 1970s, 34 percent of the people participating in a census survey in two consecutive years changed racial groups from one year to the next." Shreeve, "Terms of Estrangement," p. 58.

[10] Hoffman, "The Science of Race," p. 4.

[11] Anthony Appiah, " 'But Would That Still Be Me?' Notes on Gender, 'Race,' Ethnicity, as Sources of 'Identity,' " *Journal of Philosophy* 87, no. 10 (October 1990): 496. Appiah goes on to argue, interestingly, that there is not even something analogous to the "sex-gender distinction" on which to base the claim that there are in fact different biological races. In the case of race, biology "does not deliver something that we can use, like the sex chromosomes, as a biological essence of the Caucasian or the Negro." Appiah is not suggesting that there is, by contrast, a sexual essence, only that there is a *biological* difference (i.e., the sex chromosomes) that could provide *some* basis in biological reality for such a claim about sex, a basis that is missing altogether in the case of race.

[12] For useful summaries of the state of scientific knowledge, see the special issue of *Discover* (November 1994). Especially relevant to our discussion are James Shreeve, "Terms of Estrangement," pp. 57–63; Christopher Wills, "The Skin We're In," pp. 77–81; and Jared Diamond, "Race without Color," pp. 83–93. For the most comprehensive discussion of human genetic distribution as it relates to the issue of race among human beings, see L. Luca Cavalli-Sforza, Paolo Menozzi, and Alberto Piazza, *The History and Geography of Human Genes* (Princeton: Princeton University Press, 1994).

genetic evidence that would justify grouping people who commonly identify each other as black and white into two different races.

Shared genetic predispositions do exist among some people who are commonly identified as a race. For example: a shared genetic predisposition to sickle cell anemia exists among most Africans, which some people take as evidence for the idea that Africans are a single racial group. But some nonscientific notion of racial identity must also be operating here because the same sickle cell anemia gene is found among people in southern India and the Arabian Peninsula, but is rare among the Xhosa of South Africa and Northern Europeans.[13] The genetic disposition to Tay Sachs Disease is shared by Eastern European Jews and French Canadians, but nobody surmises that this shared genetic characteristic makes East European Jews and French Canadians into a racial group. Yet some people seem to think that the shared genetic predisposition to sickle cell anemia among (some) Africans supports the idea that they are a single racial group.

A nonscientific notion of racial identity clearly precedes the genetic evidence, which does not come close to establishing a separate and scientifically meaningful racial identity for black and white Americans, or blacks and whites more generally. The existing scientific evidence about genetic similarities and differences should lead an open-minded observer to be extremely skeptical of any usage of race that trades on the idea that human beings can be classified into distinct races for significant scientific purposes.[14] But it is not this skepticism alone that leads me to defend a distinction between race and color consciousness. If we believe in treating all human beings as equals, then we must recognize that not all kinds of color consciousness, any more than all kinds of color blindness, are created equal. By the end of this essay, I hope to show why it is important, both morally and politically speak-

---

[13] A critic quips: "Does that make Nelson Mandela and Bjorn Borg racial kin?" Steven A. Holmes, "You're Smart if You Know What Race You Are," in *News of the Week in Review, New York Times,* October 23, 1994, p. 5.

[14] The existing scientific evidence about race and intelligence is even scantier. For a useful primer and bibliographic source on the voluminous debate over the sources of intelligence, see Russell Jacoby and Naomi Glauberman, *The Bell Curve Debate: History, Documents, Opinions* (New York: Times Books, 1995).

ing, to distinguish between race and color consciousness. First, I must examine the inadequacy of the standard that many thoughtful people take to be *the* answer to racial injustice: the principle of color blindness.

PART 2. MUST PUBLIC POLICY BE COLOR BLIND?

In 1989, the school board of Piscataway High School faced budget cuts that required it to fire one of two teachers of typing and secretarial studies, Sharon Taxman and Debra Williams. Taxman and Williams had equal seniority, having been hired on the same day in 1980. Instead of flipping a coin to decide which teacher to fire, the school board decided to fire Taxman and retain Williams, the only black teacher in the school's department of business education.

This example of color conscious action is an easy target for a color blind perspective. The school board violated Taxman's right not to be discriminated against on grounds of race, and the school board's action should therefore be prohibited. It is beside any moral point admitted by a color blind perspective to say that the board may have acted consistently with the aim of overcoming racial injustice, and that this kind of action can be morally distinguished from race conscious policies that reflect "prejudice and contempt for a disadvantaged group" or increase the disadvantage of an already disadvantaged group.[15] "Discrimination on

[15] Ronald Dworkin, *A Matter of Principle* (Cambridge: Harvard University Press, 1985), p. 330. Dworkin asks whether "any race conscious distinction is always and inevitably wrong, even when used to redress inequality." His answer is that race conscious distinctions are not generally wrong because there is a difference between racial distinctions that reflect prejudice against members of a disadvantaged group (and are used to perpetuate the disadvantage) and distinctions that are designed to redress the disadvantage. This distinction is the first step in a response to advocates of color blindness who invoke Justice Harlan's admirable lone dissent in *Plessy v. Fergusson*. "Our Constitution is color-blind, and neither knows nor tolerates classes among citizens," Harlan wrote. His constitutional argument is clearly intended to avoid the legal creation or perpetuation of a caste system in which there is a "superior, dominant, ruling class of citizens" 163 U.S. 537 (1896). Although I am concerned directly with the moral rather than the constitutional question, answers to the two tend to go together.

the basis of race," Alexander Bickel wrote in a famous defense of color blindness, "is illegal, immoral, unconstitutional, inherently wrong, and destructive of democratic society. Now this is to be unlearned, and we are told that this is not a matter of fundamental principle but only a matter of whose ox is gored."[16] A contemporary critic echoes Bickel when he associates the Piscataway school board's action with "the most extreme form of racialism."[17]

If we assume an ideal society, with no legacy of racial injustice to overcome, then there is everything to be said for the color blind standard for making public policy. Fair opportunity requires that every qualified applicant receive *equal* consideration for a job on the basis of his or her ability to do the job well, not on some other basis. What counts as qualification for a job may of course be controversial, even in an ideal society (or especially in an ideal society, whose members are fully engaged in thinking through the complex demands of most jobs). But controversy over precisely what talents and attributes of individuals should count as qualifications is perfectly consistent with knowing that *some* attributes are clearly not qualifications (the eye color of doctors) and others clearly are (knowledge of human anatomy). To say that the qualifications for a job are controversial, or open to reasonable disagreement, is not to say they are arbitrary. Qualifications that are not uniquely correct are not arbitrary if they are reasonably well related to the job's social function.

That someone qualifies for a job should not be equated with meriting it, where merit is understood as a moral entitlement to the job.[18] Suppose that I have all the basic qualifications for being a professor of political philosophy, where having all the basic qualifications means being willing and able to carry out the social purposes of the position. Even were you to grant me this supposition, I would still be presumptuous to claim that I am entitled to any professorial position in political philosophy that opens up. On the other hand, I would not be presumptuous to claim that I am

---

[16] *The Morality of Consent* (New Haven: Yale University Press, 1975), p. 133.

[17] Jeffrey Rosen, "Is Affirmative Action Doomed?" *New Republic*, October 17, 1994, p. 26.

[18] For a more extensive discussion of the meaning of merit and qualification, see Michael Walzer, *Spheres of Justice* (New York: Basic Books, 1983), pp. 135–51.

entitled to equal consideration in a fair hiring process for any positions that open up for which I am basically qualified. In short, we are not owed—and we do not necessarily merit—the positions for which we are basically qualified.

To claim the contrary would hold society hostage to the job preferences of qualified people. Instead of filling jobs by what needs to be done, employers would be required to fill jobs by what qualified people wanted to do. If many more people were willing and able to teach political philosophy than to practice medicine, then they would all be entitled to a lectern even if the social need for doctors was far greater than the need for political philosophers. Although individuals do not merit the positions for which they are basically qualified, they are entitled to equal consideration with all other candidates who are basically qualified. This entitlement recognizes the right of individuals to be treated as equals when jobs are filled for social purposes.

Many of us therefore may lose out on a job for which we are fully qualified without any injustice being inflicted on us. We may even be the most qualified for a position by some reasonable but contestable understanding of what should count as the best qualifications, and still not be victim to any injustice. The claim that "I am the most qualified person for this job" is typically the strongest that any qualified person can make, but not even this claim will suffice to support a complaint of being the victim of an injustice. This is the case even if we assume—as we rarely can—that the claimant's confidence in making the claim is warranted.

Why? Qualifications for a job are relative to the social purposes of a job. Consider the example of a doctor in the general practice of medicine. Central among the social purposes of such a physician today are curing the sick, preventing avoidable illness, and alleviating physical suffering even when a cure is impossible. The social purposes of many positions, like those of a general practitioner, are also significantly open-ended. Other social purposes of general practitioners today include educating members of the public about how to live a healthier life and serving as a comfort to families of the terminally ill. This open-endedness is the first factor that contributes to there being a range of qualifications, rather than one unique set, that may reasonably be considered relevant to a job. That range is the first source of reasonable disagreement over qualifications.

The second source of reasonable disagreement is the need to rank the importance of the multiple purposes of any given position. People may reasonably disagree about how much to weigh the wide variety of technical skills that are necessary to being an excellent doctor. Similarly, we may disagree about how much relative weight to give to certain "people skills," such as the ability to communicate well with patients and get along with one's fellow doctors, once a pool of candidates is being considered all of whom have the necessary set of skills and capacities above some commonly agreed upon threshold of adequacy.

Yet a third source of reasonable disagreement lies in locating and assessing the weighted set of qualifications in actual candidates. Suppose we agree on how all the relevant qualifications for being a general practitioner in this particular medical practice should be ranked. How will we now pick the most qualified candidate for the position? Often, depending on whether or not the position is entry-level, by looking at educational credentials such as test scores and grades, letters of recommendations from teachers or past employers, and by interviewing those candidates who look most promising by these indices, which are of course imperfect. These common ways of determining who is most qualified for a position are notoriously inadequate to the task of predicting future performance. Yet this does not constitute a moral indictment of these ways. The aim of hiring—predicting future performance, not merely assessing past performance—is one that imperfect human beings cannot perfectly achieve. Extraordinarily accomplished individuals are appropriately awarded Nobel Prizes on the basis of past performance, quite independently of any expectation that they will continue their excellent work into the future. But a medical group would be not only foolish but socially irresponsible to hire physicians without trying to predict future performance, even though predicting future performance opens up the hiring process to enormous (albeit unavoidable) uncertainty.[19]

Each of these sources of reasonable disagreement is fully consistent with a nondiscriminatory policy of distributing jobs on the basis of qualifications. It is a mistake to presuppose that if only

[19] For an illuminating discussion of the controversial nature of rewards such as the Nobel Prize, see Walzer, *Spheres of Justice*, pp. 264–66.

everyone were reasonable, merit would rule and the best qualified person—by some uniquely objective standard—would be hired. In any job search conducted by fallible human beings (that is, by human beings), people of greater merit or greater qualification by some other reasonable understanding of qualification may well lose out, with no injustice being done them.

Those critiques of preferential hiring that identify the prepreferential status quo with "meritocracy" are therefore wildly misleading. I was fortunate enough not only to qualify for but also to be offered a position in political philosophy at Princeton, but I did not *therefore* merit the position. Qualifications for a job typically do not reflect a person's merit unless we simply define merit as qualifying and being chosen for a job (in which case we settle the issue by definition). Nor do most job qualifications reflect a uniquely correct interpretation of what must count as qualifications for any particular position. Nonetheless, there is likely to be substantial overlap among reasonable interpretations of job qualifications. Setting qualifications for a position is not an exercise in arbitrariness. Rather, it is an exercise in discretion, which operates against a background of considerable uncertainty as to what constitute the correct standards and how best to apply those standards in the practice of searching, identifying, and assessing qualified candidates.

The practice of preferential hiring—whether on the basis of color or some other consideration—entails something other than exercising discretion in searching for, identifying, and assessing qualified candidates. It also entails something more than taking special steps—"affirmative action"—to ensure that members of disadvantaged groups are not subject to discrimination in hiring. (I will return to consider the difference between "affirmative action," strictly speaking, and preferential hiring.) Preferential hiring goes beyond considering the qualifications of applicants. It takes into account something other than the ability of individual candidates to do a particular job well. It considers color, gender, class, family connection, or some other characteristic that is not strictly speaking a qualification for the job. By considering something other than the candidates' qualifications for the job in question, preferential hiring—as its name implies—passes over some better qualified individuals in order to serve some other social goal that is deemed worthy of pursuit, such as breaking down the racial stereotyping of high status jobs that has been created by past discrimination in society. The act of giving preference to members of the disadvantaged group denies to non-members equal consideration on the basis of their qualifications, strictly understood. Preferential hiring overrides equal consideration on the basis of qualifications in order to serve a worthy social goal. For this reason, preferential hiring is both controversial and worthy of our serious consideration. Whether preferential hiring is, all things considered, justifiable remains to be seen. But even if we cannot settle this issue, we can at least recognize that neither side in the controversy has all that is morally good on its side.

Were preferential hiring to succeed, some advocates claim, it would transfer power, status, and privilege from more to less advantaged members of society, who would then be in a position to set terms of job qualifications that would be more favorable to other, similarly less advantaged members of society. On this view, the idea of hiring people on the basis of their qualifications should be treated with great suspicion, perhaps even dismissed entirely as a moral notion, because qualifications function as a convenient fiction to support the position of already powerful and privileged people. The controversy over preferential hiring would be specious—a mere reflection of power relations—were qualifications irrelevant to carrying out important social purposes such as educating the young or curing the sick. But qualifications cannot consistently be treated as irrelevant by parents whose children would be illiterate or innumerate were it not for the talent of a good teacher, or by patients who would be dead were it not for the expertise of a good doctor.

But the advocates' view is correct in indicating that the moral terms of the debate over preferential hiring are easily skewed toward the already advantaged. Although it is not at all arbitrary to insist that teachers demonstrate literacy and numeracy, and that doctors demonstrate specialized knowledge of human anatomy and medicine, the complete set of qualifications for being a good teacher, doctor, lawyer, law-enforcement official, or corporate manager cannot be set without the exercise of a significant degree of discretionary judgment by employers, and the exercise of such discretion is subject to reasonable disagreement. Within this realm of reasonable disagreement, those members of society who now have the power to set qualifications may tend to value those qualifications that favor people similar to themselves. This is not a sufficient reason to dismiss the moral controversy over preferential hiring or reduce it to a contest of power of have-nots against haves, but it is a reason to be more suspicious of qualifications that are set by a small, privileged social group than of those that are widely scrutinized and agreed upon after deliberation by a broad spectrum of society. Far from dismissing the controversy over preferential hiring, this suspicion is one that we all can share, and it yields a constructive recommendation for setting qualifications in a way that avoids their misuse by the most powerful members of society.

The controversy over preferential hiring also cannot be dismissed, as it is by the most vehement critics, by saying that preferential hiring violates the right of the most meritorious to the jobs that they merit. Even in an ideal society without a history of racial, gender, or class discrimination, preferential hiring would not violate anyone's right to a particular job. This is because the principle of nondiscrimination, which is commonly accepted by critics and advocates of preferential hiring alike, grants no one a right to a particular job. It grants all of us a right to equal consideration for those jobs for which we are basically qualified. In an ideal society, it would be unjust to pass over individuals for jobs on the basis of something other than their inadequate qualifications (or unavoidable bad luck). In all likelihood, color would not be a qualification for any job in a just society. All hiring and firing would therefore be color blind.

But it is in our context, not the ideal one, that we must ask whether all employers are morally bound to color blindness. Suppose we begin by agreeing that in a just society, public policies would not distinguish among individuals on the basis of their color. This is our common ground, and it is critical to recognize it before we proceed into more controversial territory. A commitment to nondiscrimination underlies any publicly defensible response to racial injustice. The controversy over preferential treatment persists in this country because, despite a widely shared commitment to nondiscrimination, the United States in the 1990s does not satisfy the premise of a perspective that makes color blindness the obviously correct interpretation of what non-discrimination—or justice as fairness—among individuals demands. We should also be able to agree that color blindness itself is not a fundamental principle of justice; nondiscrimination or fairness among individuals is.

Another necessary characteristic of our common ground, which cannot be established merely by means of a political philosophy, entails an empirical assessment of the differential life chances of American citizens. I can only summarize here what many excellent empirical studies of this society confirm.[20] Ongoing racial discrimination beginning early in the life of most black Americans compounded by grossly unequal and often inadequate income, wealth, educational opportunity, health care, housing, parental and peer support—all of which are plausibly attributable (in some significant part) to a history of racial injustice—combine to deny many black Americans a fair chance to compete for a wide range of highly valued job opportunities in our society. This observation by itself does not justify—or even recommend—preferential treatment for blacks, but it should lead us to criticize any color blind perspective that collapses the fundamental principle of fairness into a commitment to color blindness. In so doing, a color blind prespective fails to leave room for according moral relevance to the fact that we do not yet live in a land of fair equality of opportunity for all American citizens—let alone in a world of fair equality of opportunity for all persons, regardless of their nationality. (The latter is an equally urgent issue that this essay cannot address.) We will never live in a land of fair equality of opportunity unless we find a way of overcoming our legacy of racial injustice.[21]

[20] See, for example, Douglas S. Massey and Nancy A. Denton, *American Apartheid: Segregation and the Making of the Underclass* (Cambridge: Harvard University Press, 1993); Christopher Jencks and Paul E. Peterson, eds., *The Urban Underclass* (Washington, D.C.: Brookings Institution, 1991); and William Julius Wilson, *The Truly Disadvantaged: The Inner City, the Underclass, and Public Policy* (Chicago: University of Chicago Press, 1987).

[21] There is almost no theory of justice—liberal, egalitarian, or libertarian—by which the United States today can be judged a just or nearly just society. My own conception of a just society would secure everybody's basic liberties (regardless of race, religion, gender, or sexual preference, for example) and also secure basic opportunities (such as a good education, adequate health care, and

The principle of nondiscrimination in hiring is a principle of fairness, which remains relevant even in societies like our own that fall far short of justice (as all societies do, although to different degrees and on different dimensions). But the policy implications of nondiscrimination are far more complex than color blindness admits. To take a person's color into account in hiring or firing, even as the decisive factor, is not in itself to engage in the practice of preferential treatment, as we can see by returning to the Piscataway case. In our nonideal context, we can say something principled in the Piscataway school board's favor by invoking the very same principle of nondiscrimination that would require color blindness in an ideal society. Nondiscrimination means that equal consideration should be given to all qualified candidates so that candidates are chosen on the basis of their qualifications, where qualifications are set that are relevant to the legitimate social purposes of the position in question.

Can color be counted as a qualification for a teaching position at Piscataway High? It is certainly reasonable to think so. It is widely accepted among advocates and critics of color blindness alike that highly selective colleges and universities may legitimately (even if not optimally) consider geographical residence as a relevant qualification for admission—being from Iowa is an added qualification for admission, for example. Suppose I think that giving any weight at all to geographical distribution in college admissions is not the best policy. I still can recognize the legitimacy of admissions officials and trustees deciding to do so despite what I believe to be best. This is a determination within the realm of discretionary authority, and a discretionary realm cannot be abolished short of instituting a society governed by an all-knowing, morally perfect philosopher king or queen. If a university like Princeton may legitimately consider the geographical

---

physical security) for everyone, provide decent jobs and child care opportunities for all adults who are willing and able to work, a substantial safety net to those unable to work through no fault of their own, and would distribute scarce, highly skilled jobs according to the principle of nondiscrimination. A just society would also empower citizens and their representatives to deliberate about the political decisions that affect their lives. A defense and elaboration of this conception of justice is in Amy Gutmann and Dennis Thompson, *Democracy and Disagreement* (Cambridge: Harvard University Press, 1996).

distribution of its students in admissions, may a school like Piscataway not consider the color of its teachers as a relevant qualification in hiring or firing?

More may be said for the qualification of color in the Piscataway case than for that of geography in the case of university admissions. But let us start with the less controversial case of rare geographical residence as a qualification for university admissions. The idea of considering a student's residence as a qualification is surely not that the student did anything to merit being from Iowa. It is that her residence—along with many other qualifications that make her basically qualified for admission (but do not give her a right to be admitted)—will contribute in some significant way to the university's educational and associational purposes.

Something similar may be said for the more controversial case of counting color as a qualification for university admissions. Despite its being more controversial, the case for counting color is significantly stronger. Were it not for the presence of black students in universities like Princeton, students and teachers alike would have far less sustained contact with significantly different life experiences and perceptions, and correspondingly less opportunity to develop the mutual respect that is a constitutive ideal of democratic citizenship. If educational institutions in a liberal democracy are to fulfill their educational purpose, they must try to cultivate not only tolerance—an attitude of live and let live (which the law enforces)—but also mutual respect (which no law can enforce)—a positive reciprocal regard based on understanding—among people with diverse life experiences and perceptions.[22] Toleration is an important precondition for mutual respect, but without mutual respect, no constitutional democracy or educational institution can live up to its potential, and no student can expect to learn as much as a university has to offer.

We are now in a better position to address the even more controversial case of color conscious firing at Piscataway. Taken at its strongest, this is not a case of preferential treatment. The Piscataway school board thought that being black was a relevant qualifi-

---

[22] A discussion of the ideal of mutual respect among citizens is found in Amy Gutmann and Dennis Thompson, "Moral Conflict and Political Consensus," *Ethics* 101 (October 1990): 64–88.

cation in a department that had only one black teacher. Why? One reason is captured by the thought that black teachers can serve as role models for both black and nonblack students. This thought is surely reasonable as long as the board did not take color as the *only* relevant qualification, but rather as one among many qualifications, which could turn out to be decisive in some cases. If the two teachers were otherwise equally qualified, as all parties to this case seem to admit, then using color as a tie-breaking qualification is justifiable. Furthermore, the use of color as a tie-breaking qualification is consistent with a policy of nondiscrimination. It is not a matter of preferential treatment precisely because color may reasonably be considered a qualification in a department that would otherwise have no black teachers. In this context, a black teacher can contribute to an educational purpose of schooling in a way that a white teacher cannot by providing a role model that breaks down a social stereotype. Being black, on this view, is directly relevant to carrying out the purpose of the teaching position. It is therefore a qualification, in the strict sense of the term. (If we do not use the term strictly, we eliminate the category of preferential hiring entirely, and thereby fail to take seriously the strongest criticisms leveled against it.)

Taxman lacked the tie-breaking qualification of being black, obviously through no fault of her own. That a qualification is unearned does not discredit it as a qualification. Many applicants to universities lack the qualification of being from Iowa (and many people who might otherwise aspire to play professional basketball lack the qualification of being sufficiently tall) through no fault of their own. Yet few people suggest that universities should not be permitted to prefer Iowans over equally qualified Californians (and the NBA to prefer tall players to short ones), even if their ideal set of qualifications would disregard geographical diversity. To criticize a hiring or admissions policy for not being the best one that could be designed is very different from claiming it to be illegitimate or unjust. Were you to think that geographical diversity should be given less weight, or even no weight, in university admissions, you could still respect the right of universities (including public ones) to use geographical diversity as a qualification. Similarly, critics of the Piscataway school board's decision should be able to recognize the reasonableness of its policy, even if they can imagine a better policy. A better policy might be one that judged the actual contribution that each teacher had made, and was likely to make in the future, to educating disadvantaged students of different colors.

The dismissive critique of the Piscataway case—as analogous to the most extreme form of racialism—illustrates a common misuse of the principle of nondiscrimination. There is a tendency, on the one hand, to accept as legitimate qualifications those attributes of individuals—including unearned characteristics such as geographical residence—that have long been considered relevant qualifications while, on the other hand, to reject color (or gender) as a qualification because it has long been illegitimately used to discriminate against individuals. This tendency is understandable; the suspicion about the misuse of race (or gender) is even morally useful to a point. But when the tendency is left unchecked, when nondiscrimination is confused with color blindness and is said to prohibit using race (or gender) as a qualification, injustice is far more likely to be served than its opposite. The unchecked tendency insulates long-established hiring and admissions practices—such as counting seniority as a qualification for hiring, or residence and legacy status as qualifications for university admissions—from critical scrutiny at the same time as it erects an insurmountable barrier to careful consideration of cases like that of the Piscataway school board, where being black is at least as relevant as seniority to the purpose of high school teaching, or as being from Iowa is to the purpose of higher education.

We do not undermine the idea of qualifications when we recognize that the set of qualifications for hiring or admissions is typically quite open-ended, even if there are boundaries beyond which it would be unreasonable to claim that someone is basically qualified to be admitted as a student to a selective university or hired as a high school teacher. Within these bounds, the setting of qualifications is rightly subject to the ever-changing results of ongoing deliberation by the broad range of people whom a democratic society legitimately authorizes to decide on admissions and hiring. In some cases, those people will be public employees, in other cases, not. But in all cases, a range of discretion may legitimately be exercised, not without public criticism, but without the results being deemed unconstitutional. The Piscataway school board's decision that Williams, by virtue of being black, had a qualification for teaching in Piscataway that Taxman lacked falls within such broad constitutional bounds.

This claim is less controversial than the claims of preferential hiring, since taken at its strongest the Piscataway case (despite the overwhelmingly negative publicity) is not a case of preferential treatment, but one in which the qualifications for a position reasonably include a person's color and being black is used to break a tie at the time of firing. The claim of preferential treatment, by contrast, is that employers may legitimately give *preference* to some *basically* qualified candidates over other *more* qualified candidates because of their color (or gender, or some other characteristic that is not tied to superior job performance). If we are considering a case of preferential hiring, then the preference would be based on reasons other than the candidates' qualifications for the job in question. (If the preference is based on a candidate's greater qualifications for the job by virtue of being black, then it is misleading to call the practice preferential hiring.) The practice of giving preference to some basically qualified candidates for a job over other better qualified candidates is what defines a policy or practice of preferential treatment and allows us to distinguish it from cases where color, gender, geographical distribution, or some other characteristic is reasonably considered a qualification for carrying out the social function of this particular job.

It is important not only to use the term "preferential treatment" in this strict sense but also to distinguish it from the more generic term, "affirmative action," which is often misleadingly used to mean preferential treatment. Affirmative action, as originally articulated, entails taking steps that would not have to be taken for members of an advantaged group in order to ensure that members of a disadvantaged group are not discriminated against. How, if at all, can preferential treatment—as distinguished from affirmative action—be justified? Once we collapse affirmative action and preferential treatment, as our contemporary public debate has done, then we cannot pose this question or clarify the controversy that surrounds the very different practices of giving preference to members of disadvantaged groups and taking positive steps that would not be necessary absent our legacy of racial injustice to prevent discrimination against them.

Many radically different arguments have been offered for and against preferential treatment, and I cannot review them all here. Instead, I focus on the morally strongest case that can be made in the context of our society for preferential treatment of black Americans. That case rests on the ideal of fairness or fair equality of opportunity, which also informs the principle of nondiscrimination. The strongest argument for preferential treatment from the perspective of anyone committed to justice as fairness is that it paves the way for a society in which fair equality of opportunity is a reality rather than merely an abstract promise. By giving preference to basically qualified black candidates over better qualified nonblack candidates, employers—especially those who control large-scale institutions—may help create the background conditions for fair equality of opportunity. How can they do so? By breaking down the racial stereotyping of jobs that has resulted from our racist past. Many scarce and highly valued jobs in our society remain racially stereotyped because of this past. In this context, even institutions that faithfully apply the principle of nondiscrimination in hiring may fail to convey a message of fair opportunity to blacks. Absent this message, hiring practices are also bound to fail the test of fair opportunity.

If preferential hiring of basically qualified blacks can help break down the racial stereotyping of jobs, then employers may legitimately consider not only a candidate's qualifications, which are specific to the job's purpose, but also a candidate's capacity to move society forward to a time when the principle of nondiscrimination works more fairly than it does today. It is reasonable to think that by hiring qualified blacks for stereotypically white positions in greater numbers than blacks would be hired by color blind employers, the United States will move farther and faster in the direction of providing fair opportunity to all its citizens. There are three ways in which preferential hiring may help move our society in this direction: by *breaking down racial stereotypes*, by *creating identity role models* for black children and, as important, by *creating diversity role models* for all citizens. Identity role models teach black children that they too can realistically aspire to social accomplishment, while diversity role models teach all children and adults alike that blacks are accomplished contributors to our society from whom we all may learn.[23] All three of these considerations—breaking racial stereotypes and creating identity and diversity role models—are of course color conscious.[24]

It is also important to note what defenders of preferential hiring practices share in common with their color blind critics. All stand opposed to hiring candidates who are unqualified, and who therefore cannot carry out their jobs well. (It should be clear that advocates of affirmative action in university admissions—as distinguished from preferential treatment—also stand opposed to admitting students who cannot graduate or remain in good academic standing. Affirmative action does not even entail admitting less qualified over more qualified students. It entails taking special steps to ensure nondiscrimination toward members of disadvantaged and underrepresented groups.) Both affirmative action and preferential hiring are no doubt subject to abuse. (The abuse of affirmative action in some cases may help account for why it is now so frequently assimilated to preferential treatment.) But neither should be dismissed as illegitimate by pointing to institutions that have admitted or hire unqualified blacks. Color blindness could be dismissed as readily by pointing to policies that, while color blind on their face, discriminate by setting qualifications—such as being the child of an alumnus or getting along well with the existing work force, which happens to be predominantly white—that are not essential to the legitimate social purposes of an institution. The abuses of both color blind and color conscious policies are avoidable by good-willed people.

If we need not be color blind, then we may be color conscious. But not all color conscious policies are defensible. By posing two

---

[23] Diversity role models also can help break down racial prejudice. "It is one thing for a white child to be taught by a white teacher that color, like beauty, is only 'skin-deep,'" as Justice Stevens wrote in his dissenting opinion in *Wygant v. Jackson*. "It is far more convincing to experience the truth on a day-to-day basis." *Wygant v. Jackson Board of Education*, 476 U.S. 287 (1986).

[24] For a defense of a similar set of purposes for affirmative action policies in the context of law school admissions and hiring, and an argument for why, given these purposes, African-Americans are the paradigmatic case that justifies affirmative action, see Paul Brest and Miranda Oshige, "Affirmative Action for Whom?" *Stanford Law Review* 47 (May 1995): 855–900.

questions, we can begin to distinguish more defensible color conscious policies from less defensible ones on the basis of widely shared values. First, how effective is the policy likely to be in moving us in the direction of a society of fair opportunity for all? The more effective a policy is in breaking down racial stereotyping and providing identity and diversity role models, the greater its justification in light of the aim of achieving a color blind society. Second, how fair is the policy, relative to the available alternatives, toward those individuals who are the most adversely affected by it? Where being a member of a disadvantaged and underrepresented minority is a qualification for a valued position, as it often is in university admissions, color conscious policies are more justifiable than where color is used to override qualifications, as it is in preferential hiring policies. Those preferential hiring policies that discriminate primarily against relatively advantaged individuals are more justifiable than those that discriminate primarily against relatively disadvantaged individuals. If a preferential hiring policy requires disadvantaged individuals to bear grossly disproportionate costs of creating a just society, a democratic society should provide some kind of compensation to those individuals. (Here is yet another reason why economic injustice toward the least advantaged individuals, regardless of their color, makes it more difficult to address racial injustice in a fair way. Something similar may be said about addressing gender injustice in a society where many well-qualified men as well as women are unemployed, or at least underemployed.) The most defensible policies that disproportionately burden a few individuals also try to find ways of compensating them for these burdens.

The most justifiable color conscious policies therefore are not likely to be the most piecemeal. The most justifiable would avoid gratuitous unfairness while they would help secure their own demise by bringing black Americans into positions of social status, economic power, and civic standing. The Piscataway plan, although clearly color conscious, is fair by both standards. Like virtually all color conscious policies, it would not bring about a society of fair equality opportunity for all Americans, even if it were generalized. The plan comes into play only in the relatively rare cases of ties in seniority and therefore, if generalized, would have a far from global effect in breaking down racial stereotyping and creating role models.[25] This surely cannot constitute a critique of the plan, since the alternative of a color blind policy would in all likelihood do even less.

Some critics who say they are otherwise sympathetic to color conscious policies reject them by pointing to all the negative publicity that has increasingly accompanied them. They suggest that color blind policies are more likely to move us in the direction of a color blind society than color conscious policies, however well-intentioned. The publicity received by the Piscataway plan was overwhelmingly negative, as critics not only point out but also help bring about. Should the plan therefore be rejected on the grounds that the negative publicity threatens to set back the cause of racial justice? I think not, because the premise of this case against the Piscataway plan—that opposition to the plan rests on the indefensible claim that it is unfair—turns out to conflict with the very principle of nondiscrimination that the critic must advocate to be consistent. If the Piscataway plan is consistent with fair equality of opportunity, then it does not make sense to set it aside on grounds that it blocks our moving forward to a society of fair equality of opportunity.

Rather than capitulate to negative publicity, it would be far better to expose the mistaken premise—that color blindness is a basic principle of justice—and to defend the common commitments to nondiscrimination and fair equality of opportunity for all that are fundamental to constitutional democracy. These com-

---

[25] Policies like Piscataway's may be subject to the criticism that "the bottom line on affirmative action is the paltriness of its material benefits." See Carol M. Swain, "A Cost Too High to Bear," *New Democrat*, May–June 1995, p. 19. But the AT&T example, which I shall discuss presently, does not support Swain's conclusion that "whatever else one may say about affirmative action policies, the actual progress they have brought has been meager indeed." We are not constrained by a "love it or leave it" approach to all affirmative action and preferential hiring programs if we can distinguish among different kinds of policies. Swain urges us to address the challenging question that conservatives pose to liberals of "whether the practical gains from these policies outweigh the resentment and pain they have caused." Without pretending to offer a calculus of costs and benefits, we can assess what can be said for and against vastly different kinds of affirmative action and preferential treatment policies. I have only begun such an assessment here. See also the interesting attempt to carve out a "middle ground on affirmative action" by Jeffrey Rosen, "Affirmative Action: A Solution," *New Republic*, May 8, 1995, pp. 20–25.

mitments can justify many color conscious policies, including the Piscataway plan. To reject color conscious policies that would otherwise be defensible because of the negative publicity (and mistaken claims of preferential treatment) that they provoke threatens to make public attacks on those policies, however weak in moral terms, politically self-fulfilling. A morally defensible democratic politics cannot afford to pursue such a strategy of capitulation.

The more citizens who accept the morality of color conscious policies, the more good is likely to come from the best of such policies. But we should not expect preferential hiring policies to become universally accepted in our society. Would we even need such policies were citizens overwhelmingly to accept them? By that time, we might already have become a society of liberty and justice for all individuals, regardless of their color. It would be paradoxical in this sense to capitulate to negative publicity about preferential hiring policies. Were it reasonable to expect little negative publicity, then it would not be necessary to support the policy. The good of overcoming racial injustice would probably have already occurred.

Even in a society where preferential hiring is highly contentious, there is reason to believe that some preferential hiring policies can have beneficial effects, on balance. Any such judgment will no doubt remain controversial, but we have no better choice than to judge the overall effects of preferential hiring on the basis of a close look at particular policies. Let us therefore consider a policy that was recognized by proponents and critics alike to be one of preferential hiring, and a massive one at that.

In the early 1970s, AT&T instituted a "Model Plan," which has been called the "largest and most impressive civil rights settlement in the history of this nation."[26] Ma Bell's mother of all preferential hiring programs was instituted in an out-of-court settlement under governmental pressure. The plan was anything but color blind, and its effects were anything but incremental. The plan applied to eight hundred thousand employees and led to an

---

[26] *EEOC v. AT&T*, 365 F. Supp. 1105 (1973) at 1108, cited by Robert Fullinwider, "Affirmative Action at AT&T," in *Ethics and Politics*, 2d ed., ed. Amy Gutmann and Dennis Thompson (Chicago: Nelson-Hall, 1990), p. 211. A fuller discussion of the AT&T case can be found in Gutmann and Thompson, *Democracy and Disagreement*.

estimated fifty thousand cases of preferential hiring over a six-year period. It gave preference to basically qualified blacks and women for management positions over white men who (everybody conceded) had better qualifications and (in many cases) greater seniority as well. The plan successfully broke down racial stereotyping of management positions and also helped integrate AT&T's work force by race and gender.[27] The plan set a timetable of six years, after which AT&T instituted a policy of nondiscrimination in hiring and firing. In this six-year period, AT&T transformed its work force, breaking down the racial and gender stereotyping of positions ranging from telephone operators to crafts workers to corporate management.

But should the small number of people passed over for positions at AT&T because of their race, most of whom are not among the most advantaged in our society, be asked to pay the entire price of remedying the effects of racial injustice?[28] Not if we can find an equally effective alternative to preferential hiring that spreads the costs more equitably. Reparations for all those blacks who have suffered from racial discrimination, paid for by a progressive income tax, would probably be a morally better policy, but it has never come close to being adopted in this country. A massive reparations policy for all black Americans coupled with full employment, health care, housing, child care, and educational policies could in all likelihood do much more to overcome racial injustice than the best preferential hiring programs—especially if these programs were designed in ways that strengthen local communities.

But would these policies have been adopted were it not for preferential hiring? (Will they be adopted if the California Civil Rights Initiative, which would outlaw state support for preferen-

[27] The plan also gave preference to men over more qualified women in non-management positions such as telephone operator, and thereby helped break down the gender stereotyping of these jobs.

[28] The costs of preferential hiring, as Michael Walzer points out, are largely borne by the next-weakest group in society. Preferential hiring, Walzer writes, "won't fulfill the Biblical prophecy that the last shall be first; it will guarantee, at most, that the last shall be next to last." Preferential hiring is nonetheless fairer as well as faster than the color blind alternative of burdening the weakest group so as to avoid burdening the next-weakest. Michael Walzer, *Spheres of Justice*, p. 154.

tial treatment programs, becomes law?) Arthur Ashe, himself no advocate of preferential hiring programs, captured the historical context in which they are morally defensible when he wrote: "No one has paid black Americans anything. In 1666, my state, Virginia, codified the conversion of black indentured servants, with limited terms of servitude, into slaves. The Emancipation Proclamation came in 1863. In my time, no one has seriously pursued the idea of making awards to blacks for those centuries of slavery and segregation."[29] In the absence of better alternatives, we can defend those preferential hiring policies that effectively move us in the direction of racially integrating our economy provided they are not gratuitously unfair to the disadvantaged individuals who are passed over. (Adding class to racial preferences is one way of avoiding gratuitous unfairness. Although class preferences are not an adequate substitute for race conscious policies, they are an important supplement to them.) Were this country to expand employment opportunities, improve education, provide health care, child care, and housing opportunities for all its citizens, regardless of their race, some preferential hiring policies might still be justifiable if they were needed to equalize job opportunities in the short run by breaking down the racial stereotyping of jobs and providing role models.[30] Even massive preferential hiring on the

[29] Arthur Ashe and Arnold Rampersand, *Days of Grace: A Memoir* (New York: Ballantine, 1993), p. 168. Ashe goes on to argue that although black Americans may be entitled to something, "our sense of entitlement has been taken too far." He argues that "affirmative action tends to undermine the spirit of individual initiative. Such is human nature; why struggle to succeed when you can have something for nothing?" (p. 170). But preferential hiring plans of the kind implemented by AT&T—and of the kind whose merits we are considering—do not give black Americans something for nothing. They give people jobs for being basically qualified and black, with the expectation that they will successfully carry out the social purposes of the position.

[30] For a counterargument, see Shelby Steele, *The Content of Our Character: A New Vision of Race in America* (New York: Harper, 1991), esp. pp. 11–125. It is hard to know how to evaluate Steele's case that affirmative action (unintentionally) demoralizes blacks and enlarges their self-doubt. We should not deny people otherwise justified benefits because of the paternalistic consideration that the benefits may demoralize them or enlarge their self-doubt. (Many successful people are tormented by self-doubt partly because they are more successful than they believe they deserve to be.) If Steele is right about the psychological effects of preferential hiring programs, there is cause for concern but not

order of AT&T's Model Plan, suitably generalized, will not itself overcome racial injustice, but neither will social welfare policies, taken by themselves. In light of our long history of racial discrimination, we should not be surprised to find that all these policies may be necessary, none alone sufficient to securing fair opportunity for black Americans.

PART 3. SHOULD PUBLIC POLICY BE CLASS CONSCIOUS RATHER THAN COLOR CONSCIOUS?

We have yet carefully to consider a proposal that promises to go a long way toward securing fair opportunity for black Americans while avoiding the pitfalls of color consciousness by shifting the focus of public policy from race to class. One advocate of "class, not race" argues that "it was clear that with the passage of the Civil Rights Act of 1964, class replaced caste as the central impediment to equal opportunity."[31] If class is the central impediment to equal opportunity, then using class as a qualification may be fairer to individuals than using race.[32] Counting poverty as a qual-

---

retraction. Without more evidence, it is hard to know whether and to what extent he is right. Steele's claim that blacks are being exempted from taking responsibility for their own educational and economic development is not sustainable against programs that consider only basically qualified candidates and expect successful candidates to perform well in their positions.

[31] Richard Kahlenberg, "Class, Not Race," *New Republic*, April 3, 1995, p. 21: "As the country's mood swings violently against affirmative action. . . , the whole project of legislating racial equality seems suddenly in doubt. The Democrats, terrified of the issue, are now hoping it will just go away. It won't. But at every political impasse, there is a political opportunity. Bill Clinton now has a chance . . . to turn a glaring liability . . . into an advantage—without betraying basic Democratic principles."

[32] Class preferences are sometimes said to be fairer because they are more individualized than race preferences. But the claim that income is an individual characteristic while race is a group characteristic makes little sense. In itself, race is no more nor less a group characteristic than income. Both generalize on the basis of a group characteristic, as do all feasible public policies. As Michael Kinsley puts it: "The generalization 'Black equals disadvantaged' is probably as accurate as many generalizations that go unchallenged, such as 'High test scores equals good doctor' or 'Veteran equals sacrifice for the nation.'" Kinsley, "The Spoils of Victimhood."

ification—on grounds that it is highly correlated with unequal opportunity, with untapped intellectual potential, and with life experience from which more affluent individuals can learn—would help blacks and nonblacks alike, but only those who are poor.[33] In addition to being fairer, its advocates claim, class preferences would be politically more feasible and therefore potentially more effective in addressing racial as well as class injustice.[34] The apparently rising tide of resentment and distrust between blacks and whites in the United States makes the call to leave race preferences behind all the more appealing.[35]

Advocates most often look to university admissions as the realm in which class should supplant color as a qualification, so it makes sense to focus on the promise of "class, not race" in this

[33] Disadvantage by race, moreover, is not remediable merely by civil or criminal penalties for people who are found guilty of racial discrimination. The costs of bringing lawsuits and the difficulty of proving discrimination are so great as to cast doubt on the argument offered by advocates of color blindness that laws against discrimination can serve as an effective deterrent. Compare Swain, "A Cost Too High to Bear," p. 20.

[34] There is also a legal case that class preferences are better than race preferences, which is based on the claim that class is not a suspect category under the Fourteenth Amendment, while race is. Class preferences therefore have the advantage of not being constitutionally suspect. The constitutional case against racial preferences, however, is largely dependent on the moral case for color blindness in our social context, which I criticized in the first two parts of this essay. Racial preferences that are used to create fair opportunity for blacks need not be suspect under the Fourteenth Amendment. Only those racial preferences that reflect prejudice against a disadvantaged group and serve to further disadvantage that group should be considered suspect. Racial distinctions that are relevant to carrying out a job well or that are designed to redress disadvantage therefore should not be deemed unconstitutional or even subject to the strictest scrutiny. See esp. Ronald Dworkin, "Reverse Discrimination," *Taking Rights Seriously* (Cambridge: Harvard University Press, 1977), pp. 223–39; and Dworkin, *A Matter of Principle*, pp. 293–334. Compare Kahlenberg, "Class, Not Race," p. 24.

[35] Advocates of class preferences also argue that class-based preferences are less likely to be stigmatizing because "there is no myth of inferiority in this country about the abilities of poor people comparable to that about African Americans." Kahlenberg, "Class, Not Race," p. 26. This is highly speculative, for once class-based preferences are instituted, they may elicit a similar myth about the inferiority of the poor. For an insightful piece of political fiction on this score, see Michael Young, *The Rise of the Meritocracy* (Baltimore: Penguin Books, 1961).

extensive and familiar realm. University admissions policies would be fairer if considerations of color were left behind, advocates argue, while considerations of class took their place. Why? Because poverty accompanied by academic accomplishment is, generally speaking, a sign of uncommon effort, untapped intellectual potential, and unusual life experiences from which more affluent students can learn.

One advocate of "class, not race" notes that "we rarely see a breakdown of [SAT] scores by class, which would show enormous gaps between rich and poor, gaps that would help explain differences in scores by race."[36] After breaking down average SAT scores by class and race, we see enormous gaps between rich and poor students. If this were all that we observed, then the shift from class to race could provide fair opportunity for black Americans, since black Americans are disproportionately poor. But when average SAT scores are broken down by class and race, we also see enormous gaps between black and white students *within* the same income groups. Moreover, the very same argument that "class, not race" advocates invoke for counting poverty as a qualification in admissions also supports the idea that being black is a similarly important qualification. The same evidence of a significant gap in SAT scores between groups—whether identified by class or color—lends support to the idea that both poor students and black students face distinctive educational disadvantages. The educational disadvantages faced by black students are not statistically accounted for by the income differentials between white and black students. This is what we should expect if (and only if) color is an independent cause of injustice in this country.

The evidence from SAT scores alone is of course insufficient to provide a full picture of either class or racial injustice, let alone its causes. But the very same kind of evidence that advocates take as sufficient to support class as a consideration for university admissions also supports color as a consideration. There is a significant gap between the average SAT scores of groups, whether those groups are defined by class, color, or both. The average combined SAT scores for black students whose parents earn between $10,000 and $20,000 is 175 points lower than the average com-

---

[36] Kahlenberg, "Class, Not Race," p. 24.

bined score for white students whose parents fall in the same income category. The gap between the average SAT scores of black and white students within this income category narrows by only 21 points out of the 196 point gap between all black and white students taking the test.[37]

As long as such gaps persist, a "class, not race" policy in university admissions will do far less to increase the higher educational opportunity of blacks than nonblacks. If selective colleges and universities reject color in order to adopt class as a consideration in admitting disadvantaged students, their student bodies would become almost entirely nonblack.[38] For colleges and universities committed to educating future leaders, this result should be as alarming as the image of an affluent, multicolored society without well-educated black leaders. It is just as doubtful that nonblack leaders in such a society could be well educated, for their education would have taken place in almost entirely nonblack universities.

Proportional representation by color in selective universities is not an ultimate goal of a just society. Fair equality of opportunity is. The problem in universities' focusing on class considerations to the exclusion of color is not disproportionality of results but unfairness, as indicated by the inconsistency in the reasoning that supports the proposed shift from color to class. The statistical evi-

[37] The gap for parental incomes between $20,000 and $70,000 is 157 points. The gap between white and black students with parental incomes over $70,000 is 144 points. The gap between white and Asian students, by contrast, increases as parental income increases. Asian students on average overtake white students once parental income surpasses about $20,000. The average SAT scores for Hispanic students range from 52 to 89 points greater than the average for black students, controlling for parental income. The source for this information about the 1990 SAT is the College Board. It is reported and discussed in Andrew Hacker, *Two Nations: Black and White, Separate, Hostile, Unequal* (New York: Scribner, 1992), pp. 139–46.

[38] Using income as a proxy for both disadvantages discriminates in favor of low-income white students and against low-income and middle-income black students. Need-based preferences in university admissions, as Jeffrey Rosen recently observed, if "honestly applied, would replace middle-class black students with lower-class white students." Rosen, "Affirmative Action: A Solution," p. 22. "This is why," as Andrew Hacker argues in *Two Nations*, "affirmative action that aims at helping blacks must take race into account" (p. 141).

dence of lower average SAT scores by income categories is taken to indicate that low-income students are disadvantaged in a way that warrants making low income a qualification. But the analogous statistical evidence of lower average SAT scores by the U.S. Census's racial categories is not taken to indicate that black students are disadvantaged in a way that warrants making color a qualification.[39]

The same statistical evidence that is used to establish the case for class as a consideration in admissions is either ignored or discounted when considering color as a consideration, and for no good reason. Some critics say that individual responsibility is undermined when black students who have lower SAT scores than nonblack students are admitted, but precisely the same argument could be made against admitting students from poor families who score lower than their more affluent peers. In both cases, the argument is extremely weak. Holding individuals responsible for their educational achievement is completely consistent with counting class *and* color as qualifications, as long as class and color are not the *only* qualifications, and individuals are not held to be *exclusively* responsible for their educational successes or failures.

The situation is therefore more complex than the "class, not race" perspective admits. In order to be admitted to a selective university, all applicants—whether they be poor, middle-class, rich, black, white, or some other color—must demonstrate unusual educational accomplishment relative to their similarly situated peers. They must also demonstrate the capacity to succeed academically, once admitted. These prerequisites to admission to a selective university ensure that individual applicants are held responsible for educational achievement. But social institutions, including universities, also share responsibility with individuals for overcoming the obstacles associated with color and class in our

[39] After observing that "SAT scores correlate lockstep with income at every increment," Kahlenberg notes that "unless you believe in genetic inferiority, these statistics suggest unfairness is not confined to the underclass." He therefore endorses giving preference to "offspring of the working poor." The same logic applies to racial disadvantage. At every income level, SAT scores vary with race. Unless you believe in genetic inferiority (for which no good evidence exists), the statistics suggest that unfairness is not confined to blacks whose parents are poor or working-class. Kahlenberg, "Class, Not Race," p. 26.

society. Why? Because to be responsible for accomplishing something entails having the effective power to do so. Individuals often do not have the power to overcome all the obstacles associated with being poor or black. Nor is responsibility a zero-sum quantity. Just because individuals are responsible for working hard does not mean that institutions are not responsible for coming to their aid, when they can thereby help equalize opportunity. It is therefore both unrealistic and unfair to expect individuals alone to overcome all the obstacles that are associated with being black or poor in our society.

The "class, not race" perspective admits half as much by urging universities to consider low income as a qualification for university admission—not the only qualification, to be sure, but a legitimate one that can justify admitting some applicants with lower SAT scores and lower high school grades and passing over other applicants with higher SAT scores and high school grades. Universities fall short of providing fair equality of educational opportunity, according to the "class, not race" perspective, to the extent that their admission policies neglect low income as an obstacle to educational achievement, and therefore refuse to pass over some applicants who score higher on these conventional indices (which do not predict future educational performance past the freshman year, let alone future career success or social leadership). The very same thing can be said about neglecting the extent to which being black is an obstacle to educational achievement in our society. The refusal to count being black as one qualification among many entails falling short of providing fair equality of educational opportunity for black students who demonstrate unusual educational achievement relative to the obstacles that they have faced. The best available evidence suggests that color and class are both obstacles, with interactive effects in the lives of a majority of black Americans.

Why, then, shift from color to class, rather than use both class and color, as independently important considerations in university admissions? The inconsistency and unfairness in substituting class for color as a qualification becomes vivid when we imagine what universities that adopt the "class, not race" perspective would effectively be saying to their applicants. To the average low-income white student, they would say—"Giving you a boost in admissions is consistent with our expectation that you have worked hard to get where you are and will continue to work hard to earn your future success." To the average low-income black student, they would say—"If we give you an added boost in admissions over the average low-income white student, we will be denying your responsibility for your lower scores and decreasing your incentive to work hard and earn your success." To average middle-income black students, they would say: "We cannot give you any boost in admissions over average middle-income white students because you no more than they have any special obstacles to overcome."

Universities could achieve consistency by refusing to consider any of the educational obstacles faced by applicants, whether they be poor or black or physically handicapped. But the price of this policy would be forsaking fair equality of educational opportunity as well as overlooking the potential for intellectual accomplishment and social leadership of individuals who have faced far greater than average obstacles to academic achievement, as conventionally measured. Yet another price of a policy of "neither class nor color" would be discounting the values—associational as well as educational—of cultural diversity on university campuses. Consistency would also require giving up all the other, nonacademic factors that the most selective universities have traditionally considered relevant in admissions, such as geographical diversity and athletic ability.

Were citizens of this society engaged in designing our system of higher education from scratch, a case might be made for counting only intellectual accomplishment in admissions. But few if any critics of counting color as a consideration in university admissions propose such a radical redesigning of our college and university system. In any case, the fairest way to such radical restructuring would not begin by giving up on color as a consideration in admissions. There are many reasons to doubt whether such a radical redesign would produce a better system of higher education than the one we now have, and there is no reason to believe that this society would democratically support such a restructuring. In this context, we cannot justify rejecting color while accepting class as one among many legitimate considerations for admissions.

What about the critics' claim that when universities give a boost to applicants above and beyond their actual educational achievements, they foster in that group of applicants a sense of irresponsibility for their (relative lack of) educational achievements? This argument from the value of individual responsibility cannot be sustained for two reasons. First, responsibility is not zero-sum. If universities assume some responsibility for helping applicants who have faced unusually great obstacles to educational achievement, they are not denying the responsibility of those applicants to work hard and demonstrate their capacity to succeed once they are admitted. (Perhaps the critics are objecting to universities that admit a high proportion of black students who cannot graduate, in which case the critics are pointing to a correctable problem, and not one that besets the strongest case for counting color as a qualification.) Second, the same argument from responsibility is rarely if ever invoked in opposition to giving a boost to low-income or physically handicapped students, even though it applies with the same (weak) force. The force of the argument is weak because responsibility for educational accomplishment is both institutional and individual. When universities share responsibility for helping students overcome educational obstacles, they do not therefore relieve them of the responsibility to succeed academically. Students who are given a boost in an admissions process still must compete for admissions, work for their grades, and compete for jobs on the basis of their qualifications.

The case for both class *and* color as considerations in university admissions is therefore strong: stronger than either consideration taken to the exclusion of the other. The "class, not race" proposal, by contrast, fails by the color blind test of fairness; it does not treat like cases alike. It discriminates against blacks by giving a boost only to students who score low because of disadvantages associated with poverty, but not to students who score low because of disadvantages that are as credibly associated with their color.[40]

[40] Giving preferences on the basis of race or class depends on the claim that admissions are not a prize for past merit but a bet on future promise along with a judgment of each student's ability to contribute to the educational institution itself. For discussion of an important distinction between the distribution of social offices, based on qualifications, and the distribution of social prizes, based on merit, see Michael Walzer, *Spheres of Justice*, pp. 135–39.

145

A more complex way of counting class as a qualification, some critics say, would avoid these inequities and thereby obviate the need to take color into account. A "complex calculus of advantage" would take into account not only parental income, education, and occupation but also "net worth, the quality of secondary education, neighborhood influences and family structure." The complex calculus of class is fairer than the simple one, which counts only income, because it considers more dimensions of disadvantage. Since blacks "are more likely than whites to live in concentrated poverty, to go to bad schools and live in single-parent homes," the complex calculus would "disproportionately" benefit blacks.[41] Its advocates say that the complex calculus not only is fair but also has a decisive political advantage over any color conscious policy: it would go almost as far toward fair equality of educational opportunity as would explicit considerations of color without calling attention to the enduring racial divisions in our society.

But the political strength of the complex calculus of disadvantage is also its weakness. By not calling attention to enduring divisions of color in our society, some suggest, we may be better able to overcome them. But it is at least as likely that we will thereby fail to make much progress in overcoming them. It is impossible to say on the basis of available evidence—and the enduring imperfections of our self-understanding—which is more likely to be the case. What we can say with near certainty is that if blacks who live in concentrated poverty, go to bad schools, or live in single-parent homes are also stigmatized by racial prejudice as whites are not, then even the most complex calculus of *class* is an imperfect substitute for also taking color explicitly into account. Perhaps the disadvantages of color can be adequately addressed by remedies that do not explicitly take color into account, but the adequacy of the complex calculus of disadvantage will then be closely related to the intention of its designers to come as close as possible to achieving the justice demanded by color as well as class consciousness.

Fairness speaks in favor of taking both class and color into account as qualifications. If politics precludes considerations of

[41] Kahlenberg, "Class, Not Race," p. 25.

color, then we are far better off, morally speaking, with a complex calculus of class than with a simple one. But we would be better off still with policies that at least implicitly recognize the independent dimension of color as an obstacle to educational achievement in our society. The color blind principle of fairness has these inclusive implications. It encourages employers and universities to consider both class and color dimensions of disadvantage (along with other dimensions, such as gender) and also to consider a wider range of qualifications for jobs and places in a university.

Even color, class, *and* gender considerations, taken together, however, would not adequately address the problem of racial injustice. None of these considerations, as commonly defended, addresses a more urgent problem: the deprivation experienced by the poorest citizens, over **30** percent of whom are black. The poorest citizens are not in a position to benefit from admissions or hiring policies that count either class or color as added qualifications. This is a weakness shared by all kinds of policies that focus on giving a boost to individuals—whatever their skin color and relative advantage to one another—who are already among the more advantaged of our society. Millions of citizens, a vastly disproportionate number of them black, suffer from economic and educational deprivations so great as to elude the admittedly incomplete and relatively inexpensive remedies of affirmative action.[42] Policies aimed at increasing employment, job training, health care, child care, housing, and education are desperately needed for all these individuals, regardless of their color. These policies, like the admissions policies we have been considering, would not give *preferential* treatment to anyone.[43] They would treat the least advantaged citizens as civic equals who should not be deprived of a fair chance to live a good life or participate as equals in democratic politics because of the bad luck of the natural lottery of birth or upbringing.

[42] As William Julius Wilson writes: "Neither programs based on equality of individual opportunity nor those organized in terms of preferential group treatment are sufficient to address the problems of truly disadvantaged minority group members." *The Truly Disadvantaged*, p. 112.

[43] For an extended and insightful defense of some of these policies, see Wilson, *The Truly Disadvantaged*. See also Massey and Denton, *American Apartheid*, esp. pp. 229–36.

Social welfare and fair workfare policies—which provide jobs that pay and adequate child care for everyone who can work—are a necessary part of any adequate response to racial injustice. They are also far more expensive than admissions and hiring policies that treat class and color as qualifications, and far more expensive than policies of preferential treatment, at least in the short run. Over time, these policies would in all likelihood more than pay for themselves. They would alleviate the increasingly expensive and widespread problems of welfare dependency, unemployment, and crime in this country. Moreover, without fair workfare and welfare policies, we cannot be a society of civic equals. Citizens will be fighting for their fair share of a social pie that cannot provide fairness for everyone; many men and women who are willing and able to work will not be able to find work that pays, and others will work full-time only to earn less, or little more than they would on welfare, while they are also unable to ensure adequate care for their children.

The political fights in such a context will invariably divide us by groups, since effective democratic politics is by its very nature group politics. To build a society in which citizens both help themselves by helping each other and help each other by helping themselves, we must be committed not only to making the economic pie sufficiently large but also to dividing it in such a way that every person who is willing to work can find adequate child care and decent work that pays.

As urgent as social welfare, workfare, and child care policies are, they would not by themselves constitute a sufficient response to racial injustice in the short run. We have seen that color conscious programs are also part of a comprehensive response to injustice, although not the most urgent (or most expensive) part. Suppose that a more comprehensive, color conscious perspective is fair. Is it feasible? An eye-opening study entitled *The Scar of Race* shows that mere mention of the words "affirmative action" elicits negative attitudes about black Americans from white Americans. After affirmative action is mentioned in the course of an interview with white citizens, the proportion of respondents who agree with the claim that "blacks are irresponsible" almost doubles, increasing from 26 percent to 43 percent. (The proportions grow from 20 to 31 percent for the claim that "blacks are lazy" and from 29 to 36 percent for the claim that "blacks are arrogant."[44]) White Americans' "dislike of particular racial policies," the authors conclude, "can provoke dislike of blacks, as well as the other way around."[45]

"Provoking dislike" is importantly ambiguous between *producing* dislike and *triggering* the open expression of it (where the dislike already preceded the mere mention of affirmative action). It is doubtful that the mere mention of affirmative action *creates* racial prejudice. More likely, it *releases greater oral expression* of preexisting racial animosity. Many white Americans seem to take the mention of affirmative action, particularly in a matter-of-fact question that opens up the possibility of their criticizing affirmative action policies, as a signal that it is acceptable to be critical not only of affirmative action but also of blacks. This is cause for concern, but the concern cannot be effectively addressed simply by relabeling affirmative action policies as something else. A good reason to avoid the term "affirmative action" is the massive confusion that surrounds its meaning. An effective and appropriate response to this confusion would be to go beyond simple sound bites, which rarely serve justice well, and distinguish between

[44] Paul M. Sniderman and Thomas Piazza, *The Scar of Race* (Cambridge: Harvard University Press, 1993), pp. 97–104. Another surprising finding discussed in this study is that larger percentages of black Americans express these negative images of blacks. Larger proportions of blacks also express positive images of blacks.

[45] Ibid., p. 104. A few pages later, Sniderman and Piazza claim that "affirmative action is so intensely disliked that it has led some whites to dislike blacks—an ironic example of a policy meant to put the divide of race behind us in fact further widening it" (p. 109). But this claim is without adequate empirical support by their study, since the divide of race must be measured by more than public opinion.

Even if affirmative action does lead some whites to dislike blacks, its beneficial effects in bringing more blacks into skilled jobs and high status positions may far outweigh its negative effects. We have many reasons to doubt that affirmative action suffices to put the divide of race behind us. But we also have many reasons to doubt that affirmative action on balance has widened the divide of race in this country, since that divide must be measured by far more than the expression of white dislike of blacks (or black dislike of whites). The vast increase in the black middle class over the decades that affirmative action has been in effect, and the decrease in the racial stereotyping of jobs, for which affirmative action is at least partly responsible, has helped narrow the divide of race.

morally better and worse policies that are color conscious. The negative reaction to the mere mention of the term "affirmative action" surely is not a sufficient reason to abandon affirmative action programs—whatever we call them—that are otherwise fair and beneficial to blacks.

Another finding of this same study suggests why it would be a mistake to oppose affirmative action only on these grounds. The popularity of programs that are perceived to help blacks is highly volatile, shifting with citizens' perception of the state of the law and the moral commitments of political leadership. When white citizens are asked for their views on a set-aside program for minorities—"a law to ensure that a certain number of federal contracts go to minority contractors," 43 percent say they favor it. But when they are told that the set-aside program for minorities is a law passed by both houses of Congress, the support significantly increases to 57 percent.[46]

Not only does the force of law seem to have the capacity to change people's minds on race matters, so does the force of moral argument. When exposed to counterarguments to their expressed positions on various policy responses to racial problems, many people switch their position in the direction of the counterarguments. This tendency is greatest for social welfare policies, such as government spending for blacks, but the tendency is also significant for affirmative action policies, where an even greater proportion of whites shift to favoring a pro–affirmative action position than switch to an anti–affirmative action position when exposed to counterarguments to their original positions. Twenty-three percent of white respondents shift from a negative to a positive position on affirmative action, compared to 17 percent who shift in the opposite direction.[47]

Moral argument and political leadership, as this study vividly indicates, make a significant difference in public opinion on race matters. This is potentially good news for deliberative democracy. Were we to make our politics more deliberative, we would also—in all likelihood—increase the potential for bringing public policy and color consciousness more in line with the force of moral arguments. There are no guarantees, of course, about where the force

[46] Ibid., pp. 131–32.   [47] Ibid., p. 148.

of argument will lead citizens and public officials on these complex issues. But as long as the potential exists for changing minds through deliberation, citizens and public officials alike have good reason—moral as well as prudential—not to endorse public policies merely because they conform to public opinion polls. "New majorities can be made—and unmade," Paul Sniderman and Thomas Piazza conclude. "The future is not foreordained. It is the business of politics to decide it."[48]

All the more reason to approach the political morality of race with renewed openness, at least as much openness as ordinary citizens evince in extended discussions of racially charged issues, which include most issues of our public life. Unless we keep the aim of overcoming racial injustice at the front of our minds and at the center of our democratic deliberations, we shall not arrive at an adequate response to racial injustice. I do not pretend to be able to provide that response, or even anything close to it in this essay. But there is value in keeping democratic doors open to exploring new possibilities and to changing minds, including our own, as our deliberations on these issues continue. Only if we keep the aim of overcoming racial injustice at the center of our deliberations about social justice can we realistically hope to develop into a democracy with liberty and justice for all.

PART 4. WHY NOT AIM FOR PROPORTIONAL REPRESENTATION BY RACE?

Effective deliberations about racial injustice cannot rely only on courts, although courts are an important forum of fairness in our constitutional democracy. Legislatures are a far more powerful forum, which the least advantaged citizens can least afford to

[48] Ibid., p. 165. Sniderman and Piazza are far less certain about this conclusion vis-à-vis what they call the "race conscious agenda," but their findings appear to hold for affirmative action as well as what they call social welfare and fair housing issues. The minority set-aside program certainly counts as preferential treatment, which is part of what Sniderman and Piazza are calling affirmative action. The positive shift in white support of a minority set-aside program upon learning that it has the sanction of law turns out to be among the more striking shifts in opinion that Sniderman and Piazza report.

neglect. What legislation comes out of legislatures depends on whose votes go into electing legislators. Whose votes go in depends not only on who votes but also on how electoral districts are designed.

Black voters in North Carolina constitute approximately 20 percent of the state's electorate. Until the recent redistricting plan was put into effect, they had not elected a black representative to the United States Congress since Reconstruction, and not for lack of trying. The vast majority of white voters voted as a bloc, and handily defeated the candidates supported by most black citizens, who also voted as a bloc. The new redistricting plan changed this situation. Critics say that the change is for the worse because it tries to ensure race proportionate representation, and in so doing not only violates the equal voting rights of individual citizens but also undermines the aim of achieving better results for black citizens. The redistricting plan is morally defensible, I shall argue, but not on grounds that it ensures race proportionality in representation.

Facing the need to redistrict after the 1990 census, having gained a twelfth seat in the United States House of Representatives, the North Carolina state legislature approved a reapportionment plan with one majority-black district. When the U.S. Attorney General found that plan in violation of the Voting Rights Act, the legislature approved a revised plan with a second majority-black district designed in a way that preserved as many districts of incumbents as possible. The most widely publicized feature of the plan was its newly created Twelfth District with a 53.34 percent black voting age population. The Twelfth District stretches for 160 miles through ten counties in a band often no wider than the Interstate Highway 85, linking the historically black parts of Durham, Greensboro, Winston-Salem, and Charlotte.[49]

The Twelfth District's shape is famous largely because it features in the Supreme Court's 5 to 4 decision in *Shaw v. Reno*. Writing for the majority, Justice O'Connor remanded the decision back to the district court, on grounds that a "bizarrely"

[49] *Shaw v. Hunt*, United States District Court for the Eastern District of North Carolina, Raleigh Division, 1994 U.S. Dist. LEXIS 11102 (August 1, 1994).

shaped majority-black district should be subject to stricter constitutional scrutiny than a merely "irregularly" shaped majority-
black district. O'Connor's opinion is at least as convoluted as the
district that it subjects to strict scrutiny. The extraordinary shape
of the district, O'Connor suggests, calls attention to its race proportionality rationale, which is morally and constitutionally suspect.[50] The plan and its race proportionality rationale, she argues,
assume that "members of the same racial group . . . think alike,
share the same political interests, and will prefer the same candidates at the polls."[51] If a government assumes that the political
interests of its citizens are given by their racial identities, then my
interests and yours can be virtually represented by anyone who
shares our racial characteristics since my being white and your
being black (by assumption) determines our different political interests. This denies each of us our individuality along with our
civic freedom as citizens.

The logic of race proportional representation says that if 20
percent of the North Carolina electorate is black, then 20 percent
of the legislature should be elected by blacks, no more, no less.
One problem with race proportionality is that it virtually guarantees majority tyranny in the United States, even as it seeks to
lessen its force by reducing the monopoly that white citizens once
had on political power. Critics like Justice O'Connor neglect to
mention, however, that race proportionality is better than the
greater preponderance of white power that preceded it. But our
options are not limited to white power and race proportionality,
nor is achieving race proportionality in representation the best defense of the North Carolina plan.

The North Carolina plan gives black citizens greater prospects
of electoral success than they have had in the past. And it gives

---

[50] O'Connor also suggests that the "irrational" shape of the second majority-
black district signals the intent to "*segregate* voters into separate voting districts
because of their race" [emphasis added]. Yet the Twelfth District is not segregated. In fact, it is more integrated than many electoral districts that have passed
moral and constitutional muster. The redistricting plan also conforms to "one
person, one vote," and it does not deny white citizens a fair opportunity to elect
the representatives of their choice. See *Shaw v. Reno*, 509 US (1993), 125 L Ed
2d 511.

[51] Ibid.

them greater prospects in two senses. First, they are better able to elect a black representative, if they so choose. Call this the prospect of descriptive representation. Second, they are better able to pass legislation that is favorable to their interests and would help move this country in the direction of overcoming racial injustice. Call this the prospect of substantive representation. While no one doubts that the North Carolina plan increased the prospects of descriptive representation, many critics question whether the prospect of increased descriptive representation comes at the cost of decreasing the prospect of substantive representation. The best studies now available suggest that substantive representation tracks descriptive representation quite closely in the eight Southern states (Alabama, Georgia, Louisiana, Mississippi, North Carolina, South Carolina, Texas, and Virginia) that have been the most affected by redistricting plans to comply with the Voting Rights Act.[52]

The prospect of greater descriptive and substantive representation of black voters provides good reason to recommend the North Carolina plan over what existed before, not because blacks "think alike, share the same political interests, and will prefer the same candidates at the polls" but because blacks—whether acting as citizens or as legislators—are more likely (as a matter of contingent, historical fact) to place the interest of overcoming racial injustice near the top of their political agenda. A defense of the North Carolina redistricting plan assumes only that blacks are on average more aware than whites of our mutual (moral) interest in overcoming racial injustice, that they are more disadvantaged by the persistence of racial injustice and (therefore) more likely to give this interest the priority that it warrants. This defense of the North Carolina plan does not assume that black citizens will support the same candidates at the polls. Nor does it assume that only black legislators will serve the interests of black citizens. It assumes only that, in light of the urgency of overcoming racial injustice and the greater perception of that urgency among black citizens, black citizens should have greater prospects of electoral success than they have had in the past or than they now have.

[52] For an excellent summary of these findings, see Richard H. Pildes, "The Politics of Race," *Harvard Law Review* 108, no. 6 (April 1995): 1376–92. Cf.

Black citizens—although as varied in political views and interests as whites—tend to support programs that improve opportunities in education, employment, health care, housing, and child care for individuals in need far more than do whites. Black citizens also distrust government more than do white citizens, perceiving it to be "white-run" in a way that neglects their basic interests in overcoming massive "unemployment, poverty, inferior educational opportunities, poor health care, and the scourge of drugs."[53] Expanding the electoral influence of black citizens is a way to keep the aim of overcoming racial injustice at the front of our political minds and at the center of our democratic deliberations.

The electoral influence of black citizens would be most effectively expanded by reforms that encourage the formation of cross-racial coalitions. But there is ample evidence that majority-white districts in the South rarely form cross-racial coalitions. Quite the contrary; as the black voting population in Southern electoral districts increases from a small to a sizable minority (approaching and exceeding 40 percent), the district tends to become more racially polarized, and white voters tend to form tighter, all-white coalitions, electing white representatives whose politics do not appeal to black voters. There are barely a handful of cases that are exceptions to this empirically based rule. The rule refutes the critics' claim that a morally difficult trade-off exists between descriptive and substantive representation of black citizens in those states where redistricting battles are being most fiercely fought.[54] Unfortunately, nobody has yet figured out a way to achieve the democratic ideal of electoral redistricting in this context: one that leads to mutually respectful deliberation across racial lines and the creation of cross-racial coalitions in which black citizens have an effective chance of swinging close elections. Were a redistricting plan available that would create such democratic deliberation across racial lines, it would be preferable to the North Carolina plan.

Abigail M. Thernstrom, *Whose Votes Count?* (Cambridge: Harvard University Press, 1987).

[53] Carol M. Swain, *Black Faces, Black Interests: The Representation of African Americans in Congress* (Cambridge: Harvard University Press, 1993), pp. 7–11.

[54] Pildes, "The Politics of Race," pp. 1376–90.

In the meantime, the North Carolina plan has a lot to recommend it over the available alternatives. It increases the effective electoral voice of black citizens. And it does so in a way that does not presuppose that black citizens share the same comprehensive perspective on politics. But it recognizes that blacks on average tend to give greater political primacy than white citizens to overcoming the ongoing effects of racial injustice.[55] There is nothing illiberal or undemocratic about this recognition.

The North Carolina plan gave greater influence to black voters than was previously the case. If a justifiable aim of such a plan is to help overcome racial injustice in legislative results, then the redistricting plan would have been even better had it given black voters a greater than proportionate influence over electoral outcomes. As long as racial injustice in legislative results remains a problem, we cannot rest content with reforms that guarantee citizens equal voting power—where equal voting power is the capacity of every individual citizen to cast an equally weighted vote.[56] The guarantee of equal voting power is constitutionally essential, and uncontroversially so, although the various ways in which it can be satisfied still provoke public controversy. (This is a good example of how the unfamiliar tends to be more controversial than the familiar, even when it is no less morally problematic.) Any number of votes equally distributed among citizens can satisfy the equal power requirement for vote distribution. "One person, one vote" is the most common way of satisfying the requirement, but it is not the uniquely legitimate way of providing equal voting power to all. "One person, seven votes" in a multimember district also secures equal voting power to citizens.

To have equal voting power is an important part of what it means to be treated as a civic equal. Why? Because equal voting power *publicly expresses* the idea of our civic equality. But equal voting power does not go as far as electoral reform can legiti-

---

[55] For a useful summary of the empirical evidence that supports these presuppositions, see Swain, *Black Faces, Black Interests*, chap. 1. Swain's study also lends empirical support to the beneficial results that can come from building cross-racial coalitions, but how willing white voters are to form such coalitions in some states remains an open question.

[56] See Charles Beitz, *Political Equality* (Princeton: Princeton University Press, 1989), p. 9.

mately go to protect black Americans against unjust results in legislation.[57] In choosing among alternative ways of equalizing voting power, all of which publicly express the idea of civic equality, it makes moral (as well as constitutional) sense to invoke the aim of protecting against racial injustice in legislative outcomes.[58] This aim favors those redistricting plans that increase the effective influence of black voters while preserving everyone's equal voting power over those plans that only secure everyone's equal voting power.

A critic might argue that what counts as racially unjust results in legislation is a matter of partisan politics and therefore cannot be a legitimate consideration in redistricting. The critic is surely correct in pointing out that there are many partisan disagreements about what counts as racially unjust results in legislation. But these partisan disagreements do not discredit the aim of reducing racially unjust results by redistricting. All parties can agree that they have a responsibility to avoid racially unjust results in legislation, and all can deliberate about what electoral designs best protect against such results just as they deliberate about whether and how to protect incumbents, which is a far less urgent—and no less partisan—consideration. Both considerations should be subject to the side constraint of securing equal voting power: a redistricting plan would be illegitimate were it to deny citizens the right to cast an equally weighted vote. But the North Carolina plan does not violate this side constraint.

We cannot of course create electoral schemes that *guarantee* just results in legislation, but we can distinguish better from

[57] See ibid., esp. pp. 8–11; and Judith N. Shklar, *American Citizenship: The Quest for Inclusion* (Cambridge: Harvard University Press, 1991), pp. 25–62.

[58] Although "one person, one vote" is one way of distributing voting power equally, it may not be the best voting rule once the aim of reducing racial injustice in electoral outcomes is taken into account. There are many legitimate ways of equally distributing the power to vote. In a multimember district with an at-large election for seven city council positions, for example, "one person, seven votes" recognizes citizens as civic equals and satisfies the standard of equal voting power. This voting scheme is what Lani Guinier calls "one vote, one value." For her detailed defense, see "Groups, Representation, and Race Conscious Districting: A Case of the Emperor's Clothes," *The Tyranny of the Majority: Fundamental Fairness in Representative Democracy* (New York: Free Press, 1994), pp. 119–56.

worse electoral designs—all of which honor the equal voting power of citizens—by judging as best we can which are more likely to help overcome racial injustice in electoral outcomes. Relative to the status quo ante, the North Carolina plan moved in this direction.[59] Relative to an ideal deliberative democracy that encourages the building of multicolor coalitions in both electoral districts and legislatures, the plan is far from perfect, as both advocates and critics can acknowledge. But the ideal may not be realizable by any electoral redistricting plan, and certainly not by one that takes the protection of incumbents as a legitimate aim. The major shortcoming of the North Carolina plan is not the "bizarre" shape of the Twelfth District but the ordinary scheme of protecting incumbents at (almost) any cost, which Justice O'Connor's opinion apparently took for granted.[60]

Little more than a year after deciding *Shaw v. Reno*, the Su-

---

[59] It also conforms to a credible interpretation of the Voting Rights Act of 1965 and the Voting Rights Amendments of 1982, on the legal bases of which the Attorney General rejected the first plan, which had only one majority-black district. The Voting Rights Act explicitly aims to protect against *racial discrimination* in voting and representation. The Act requires, for example, that black citizens not have "less opportunity than other members of the electorate to participate in the political process and to elect representatives of their choice." See *Public Law 97–205, 97th Congress* ("The Voting Rights Act Amendments of 1982").

[60] Just as this book goes to press, the Supreme Court has decided in twin five-to-four rulings to invalidate four majority-minority electoral districts, three in Texas (two majority-black and one majority-Hispanic, in the case of *Bush v. Vera* (no. 94-805), and one (the very same Twelfth) majority-black district in North Carolina, in the case of *Shaw v. Hunt* (no. 94-923). Justice O'Connor's plurality opinion in *Bush v. Vera* states the following constitutional standard of harm: "Significant deviations from traditional districting principles, such as the bizarre shape and noncompactness demonstrated by the districts here, cause constitutional harm insofar as they convey the message that political identity is, or should be predominantly racial." The fact that no black representative from North Carolina had been elected to Congress between 1901 and 1992 and no majority-white Texas district had ever elected a minority representative to either the State Senate or the United States Congress surely makes it credible to claim that political identity in North Carolina and Texas is as predominantly racial as it is predominantly anything, even if one concurs with Justice O'Connor that it ideally should not be. Our discussion focuses on the political morality rather than the constitutionality of redistricting along racial lines, but the two sets of considerations are intertwined—as is evident in the various opinions in these cases.

preme Court handed down another hotly contested 5-to-4 decision in a redistricting case, *Miller v. Johnson*.[61] This case comes from Georgia and features a new Eleventh District, which spans a 260-mile-long corridor from the outskirts of Atlanta to Savannah.[62] Writing for the majority, Justice Kennedy explicitly denied that the bizarre shape of a majority-black district triggers the need for strict scrutiny. The distinction on which the Court's majority decision now relies is not between the bizarrely and merely irregularly shaped districts that may result from the redistricting process but rather between a partisan process that uses race as a "predominant" factor and one that uses race as merely one important factor among others in creating new district lines. The majority decision found that the Georgia legislature had used race impermissibly because it was the predominant factor in creating the Eleventh District.

The majority's reasoning in *Miller v. Johnson* is considerably clearer than it was in *Shaw v. Reno*, but it still falls short of making a moral (or constitutional) case against color conscious redistricting. "Just as the state may not, absent extraordinary justification, segregate citizens on the basis of race in its public parks, buses, golf courses, beaches, and schools," Justice Kennedy writes, so it "may not separate its citizens into different voting districts on the basis of race."[63] But the analogy with segregated facilities is misleading. Georgia's redistricting plan does not prevent black and white citizens from living, playing, traveling, and learning together, however they see fit. Segregated public parks, buses, golf courses, beaches, and schools curtail the basic liberties of citizens and deny their equal standing as citizens. Color conscious redistricting does not curtail any citizen's basic liberty to cast an equally weighted vote in an election. Nor does it deny any citizen's civic equality or equal standing before the law.

The new, majority-black Eleventh District—unlike segregated parks, buses, golf courses, beaches, and schools—includes both black and white citizens on strictly equal terms. It denies no one the equal status and equal voting power of a democratic citizen.

---

[61] *Miller v. Johnson*, no. 94–631, 1995 U.S. LEXIS 4462 (June 29, 1995).

[62] Linda Greenhouse, "Justices, in 5–4 Vote, Reject Districts Drawn with Race the 'Predominant Factor,'" *New York Times*, Friday, June 30, 1995, pp. A1, A23.

[63] *Miller v. Johnson*, at 21.

Its defensible aim is not segregation, but greater concentration of the voting strength of black citizens than previously existed in Georgia so as to give black citizens a more effective voice in legislative politics. Concentrating black voting strength in a few districts may not be the best way to increase the effective voice of black citizens in democratic politics—but it is better than the status quo and does not violate anyone's basic rights to due process or equal protection.

Like the North Carolina plan, the Georgia redistricting plan is not optimally designed to increase the influence of black voters, because the protection of incumbents is taken for granted. But the aim of increasing the influence of black voters itself is no less legitimate, indeed more urgent, under these circumstances. The aim cannot meaningfully be said to segregate races, any more (or less) than the many redistricting plans that concentrate Republicans (or WASPS) in some districts and Democrats (or recent immigrant groups) in others can meaningfully be said to segregate these groups. In her concurring opinion in *Miller v. Johnson*, Justice O'Connor expresses a concern of fairness that redistricting that increases the legislative strength of black citizens not be treated "less favorably than similar efforts on behalf of other groups" (such as ethnic minorities).[64] If we heed this concern of equal protection in a political system that has routinely concentrated the electoral strength of relatively cohesive minorities, we should support color conscious redistricting that increases the influence of black voters in legislative politics.

As long as we do not object—as Justice O'Connor does not—to the concentrated electoral influence of other groups, we cannot consistently and fairly stop short of recognizing the legitimacy of color conscious redistricting, even if the results of color conscious redistricting are not ideal from our political perspective. The only consistent way of opposing color conscious redistricting would require overturning all previous districting efforts whose aim and effect has been to give cohesive political groups concentrated electoral influence. Few if any critics propose this course of action, nor do any justify singling out blacks as a group whose electoral influence may not be increased by redistricting. To single blacks out is to treat them unfairly.

[64] Ibid., at 52.

Justice Kennedy's objection to the use of race as a predominant factor in redistricting rather than as one among many factors offers no moral reason to single out color as an impermissible factor, whether it be predominant or part of a plurality of considerations. The criterion, some commentators have proposed, is meant to suggest that singling out race as a predominant factor constitutes an "expressive harm," analogous to the harm that would be committed by a statute that does nothing more than declare the United States a "Christian nation."[65] There are at least two serious problems with this analogy. First, the redistricting efforts that created North Carolina's Twelfth and Georgia's Eleventh Districts did not declare race a predominant factor. In both cases, not only did incumbency clearly constrain the redistricting designs but the designs were also on their face respectful of the constitutional requirement of securing equal voting power for every citizen. Second, unlike a statute that actually declares the United States a Christian nation, these redistricting plans did not make any unconstitutional declaration. If there is an unconstitutional meaning in the redistricting plans, it must be read into them. But one plausible and publicly accessible reading of the plans is that they aim to increase the electoral influence of black voters while protecting as many incumbents as possible. On this meaning, the plans are not remotely analogous to a statute declaring us a Christian nation. The expressive content of the redistricting plans is both morally and constitutionally defensible as a statute declaring us a Christian nation is not.

Other criticisms of the redistricting plans are no doubt possible, but the question before us is not whether the plans are the best that could possibly be devised but rather whether color conscious redistricting is morally and constitutionally legitimate. I have suggested that, were it possible, color conscious redistricting that encourages the building of cross-racial coalitions would be

[65] Jacob Levy has suggested this possible interpretation of Justice Kennedy's distinction based on an insightful analysis of *Shaw v. Reno* by Richard Pildes and Richard Niemi, "Expressive Harms, 'Bizarre District,' and Voting Rights: Evaluating Election-District Appearances after *Shaw v. Reno,*" *Michigan Law Review* 92, no. 3 (December 1993): 483–587. Pildes and Niemi write that "*Shaw* therefore rests on the principle that, when a government appears to use race in the redistricting context in a way that subordinates all other dominant values, the state has impermissibly endorsed too dominant a role for race" (p. 509).

better than plans that concentrate blacks very heavily in only a very few districts, often in an effort to protect as many incumbents as possible. But I have also suggested that color conscious redistricting, even if it falls short of an ideal of deliberative democracy, is a more promising means of moving us in the direction of overcoming racial injustice than preserving the status quo.[66]

Defensible redistricting plans, designed in a way that helps overcome racial injustice in legislative outcomes, may sometimes coincidentally also achieve race proportionality in representation by black legislators, but this is not the ultimate or most defensible aim of color conscious redistricting.[67] The aim most worthy of democratic support is to help overcome racial injustice by means of increasing the prospects of electoral success for black citizens and, whenever possible, by encouraging cross-color coalitions.[68]

[66] Overcoming racial injustice in legislation is not *the only critical aim of electoral reform*, but it is one critical aim, and perhaps the dominant one. Had the Court or the North Carolina legislature made a case for another aim (such as overcoming poverty or unemployment for all citizens) being dominant and conflicting with the redistricting scheme that increases the effectiveness of black citizens, then the relative moral urgency of the other aim would need to be considered. Making the votes of black citizens more effective by redistricting would probably also support these and many other morally urgent aims.

[67] I should emphasize that the argument for increasing representation of black citizens is specifically addressed to overcoming the problems of racism in the United States. Group representation schemes that are designed primarily for black Americans may be justified even if group representation for every disadvantaged group would be impracticable. The slippery slope argument against race conscious redistricting that claims a consequent need to increase the electoral prospects of every other ascriptive group in the United States is a non sequitur. No other ascriptive group with the exception of Native Americans (for whom truly exceptional arrangements concerning sovereignty and governmental structure have been made) is as greatly disadvantaged by virtue of an ongoing legacy of racism in this country.

[68] This argument connects a concern for overcoming racial injustice with a call for more effective representation of blacks in American politics. It rests on liberal democratic ideals and rejects any essentialist conception of race. Compare Iris Marion Young's more general call to provide "mechanisms for the effective recognition and representation of the distinct voices and perspectives of those of its constituent groups that are oppressed or disadvantaged" in *Justice and the Politics of Difference* (Princeton: Princeton University Press, 1990), p. 184. The claim that a close connection obtains between greater representation of a disadvantaged group and better legislative outcomes is open to reasonable demo-

PART 5. WHAT'S MORALLY RELEVANT ABOUT RACIAL IDENTITY?

I have saved for last the deepest challenge to color conscious policies. It is the worry that they perpetuate a troubling kind of consciousness, race or color consciousness, which it should be their purpose to destroy. Even if this worry does not lead us to endorse a color blind perspective, it does introduce a sobering note into any call for color conscious policies. "The harm of perpetuating race consciousness," as David Wilkins puts it, "must be balanced against the harm of ignoring reality."[69]

Before we begin the balancing, however, we need to be clear about the harm of perpetuating color consciousness. Not all kinds of color consciousness are equally troubling. A common kind— which I shall call race consciousness to distinguish it from a more contingent kind of color consciousness—is troubling, exceedingly so. Race consciousness is the kind of consciousness that presumes the existence of separate human races and identifies race with essential natural differences between human beings that are morally relevant. Either phenotypical differences such as facial features and skin color are accorded moral significance in themselves or, more often, they are considered indicative of some deeper, morally significant differences between blacks and whites.

Contingent color consciousness, or what we can simply call color consciousness for short, rejects race as an essential, natural division among human beings and also rejects the idea that there are morally relevant differences that correspond to racial divisions among human beings. Color consciousness entails an awareness of the way in which individuals have historically come to be identified by superficial phenotypical differences—such as skin color

---

cratic disagreement, but it is quite plausible on its face. See also Lani Guinier, "The Triumph of Tokenism: The Voting Rights Act and the Theory of Black Electoral Success," *Michigan Law Review* 89, no. 5 (March 1991): 1077–1154; and "No Two Seats: The Elusive Quest for Political Equality," *Virginia Law Review* 77, no. 8 (November 1991): 1461–1513.

[69] David B. Wilkins, "Two Paths to the Mountaintop? The Role of Legal Education in Shaping the Values of Black Corporate Lawyers," *Stanford Law Review* 45 (July 1993): 2004.

and facial features—that serve as the bases for invidious discriminations and other injustices associated with race. Were we to lack color consciousness of this contingent kind, we would be blind to a basic source of social injustice. Just as some kinds of color conscious policies are better than others from a moral point of view, so too are some kinds of color consciousness.

We can distinguish these two kinds of consciousness more clearly by returning to the idea of race as a correlate of a large cluster of genetically based distinctions among human beings. Race consciousness has repeatedly been used to rationalize all sorts of injustice, including some of the worst atrocities known to humankind. The rationalization—these people are members of a different race, therefore we need not treat them simply as fellow human beings—does not rely on logic or morality any more than it does on science. The belief that black and white Americans are genetically distinguishable races of human beings, even were it true, could not by itself justify depriving a single human being of a single basic liberty or opportunity available to other human beings.

In principle, the dignity of human beings and their civic equality does not depend on our exposing the fiction of racial identification. But we ignore the fiction at our moral and political peril. It is not enough to demonstrate as a matter of moral logic that even if there were different races among human beings as we now know them, none of the invidious discriminations associated with race consciousness would be justified. The psychology of identifying only with members of "one's own race" has the capacity to overwhelm the logic of a universalistic morality of mutual respect among *all* human beings, a morality that presupposes our equality or dignity as human beings.

But neither is it enough to demonstrate the scientific fiction of race, and let the morality of mutual respect speak for itself. Some nonracialist ways of identifying and distinguishing ourselves, by nationality and ethnicity, for example, do not rest on any scientific fiction, and may even recognize their own historical contingency and social construction, but they nonetheless fuel a sense of superiority, hostility, distrust, and disrespect among groups. This sense of animosity among groups typically leads to unjust and undemocratic discriminations in the distribution of basic liberties

164

and opportunities. Without believing that their separateness and superiority is racially based, members of cultural groups can feel separate and superior in ways that they wrongly assume to warrant restrictions on other people's basic life chances.[70] Because socially constructed cultures that are perceived as such may also be infused with a sense of superiority and disrespect toward outsiders, we cannot assume that the demands of fairness will win out once the fiction of race is exposed. Race consciousness is therefore not unique in supporting a group psychology that has morally troubling effects.

Nonetheless, race consciousness has so pervaded our national history and so repeatedly rationalized injustice that the rationalization as well as the injustice need to be exposed. The rationalization, worth repeating because its moral bankruptcy is most striking when exposed—these people are members of a different race, therefore we need not treat them as equals, as our fellow human beings—relies not on logic but on human weakness, maybe the most profound human weakness other than our mortality, and certainly one of our gravest moral weaknesses. Unlike our mortality, our tendency to associate ourselves as distinct races among human beings and to care only, or even primarily, for people who live with us and look like us is our responsibility to control.

The very act of identifying with people of "one's own race" simply by virtue of their being of one's own race has had the psychological effect of undermining mutual identification among individual human beings. (Something similar can be said about some national and ethnic identifications.) Absent our mutual identification, we are likely to be less motivated to ensure that justice is done for people who look and act differently from ourselves.[71] Defying logic but catering to human weakness, racial

[70] For two accounts of nationalism that differentiate among those nationalisms that are hostile to others and those that are compatible with a universalistic morality (such as justice as fairness), see Yael Tamir, *Liberal Nationalism* (Princeton: Princeton University Press, 1993); and James Kellas, *The Politics of Ethnicity and Nationalism* (New York: St. Martin's Press, 1991).

[71] Quite apart from the loss in moral motivation that is the likely outcome of identification by race, the lack of identification itself is troubling, especially (but not only) for people who share a society together. Adrian Piper writes illumi-

identification has the capacity to rationalize injustice by a process of transference analogous to the one described by Frederick Douglass over a century ago:

> The evils most fostered by slavery and oppression are precisely those which slaveholders and oppressors would transfer from their system to the inherent character of their victims. Thus the very crimes of slavery becomes slavery's best defense. By making the en-slaved a character fit only for slavery, they excuse themselves for refusing to make the slave a free man. A wholesale method of ac-complishing this result is to overthrow the instinctive conscious-ness of the common brotherhood of man.[72]

Even if consciousness of our common humanity is not instinctive but learned or, as is most likely, partly instinctive and partly learned, the persistence of race consciousness (as distinguished from color consciousness) has the psychological tendency to transfer the moral evil of discriminatory institutions into pre-sumptions of morally relevant differences among individuals. The transference undermines not only mutual identification but also mutual respect among human beings.

Moral matters become more complicated, as critics like Douglass also recognized, because even race consciousness of this problematic sort can be double-edged. When race consciousness flows from the experience of identification as a member of an op-pressed group, it also serves to unite members of the group to struggle against their oppression. In addition, race consciousness

---

natingly that "the ultimate test of a person's repudiation of racism is not what she can contemplate *doing* for or on behalf of black people, but whether she herself can contemplate calmly the likelihood of *being* black. If racial hatred has not manifested itself in any other context, it will do so here if it exists, in hatred of self as identified with the other—that is, as self-hatred projected onto the other." The manifestation of racial identification in the aversion of white Ameri-cans to the idea of being black themselves is very troubling quite apart from the lack of moral motivation to do something substantial to improve the circum-stances of people of another color. See Adrian Piper, "Passing for White, Passing for Black," *Transition* 2, no. 4 (1992): 19. See also M. C. Dawson, *Behind the Mule* (Princeton: Princeton University Press, 1994).

[72] *The Life and Writings of Frederick Douglass*, vol. 2, ed. Philip S. Foner (New York: International Publishers, 1950), p. 295.

among oppressed peoples often leads to the creation of vibrant and valuable cultures (importantly plural, not singular), as it has in American history. These cultures, while associated with the experience of oppression, take on a highly valued life of their own, primarily but not only for the descendants of the people whose oppression first and foremost informed the culture. One important challenge of liberation movements—a challenge addressed by Martin Luther King, Jr., in a particularly compelling way—is to decouple racial identity from the color consciousness that is necessary for unity in the struggle against racial oppression, and for an ongoing appreciation of the vibrant cultures associated with the history of racial oppression.

The decoupling, if successful, carries with it at least two important advantages. The first and most direct advantage is the exposing of a dangerous fiction, that of racial identity. Black Americans who reject the notion of racial identity refuse to live the lie that their oppressors have attempted to force upon them. This in itself is a significant triumph against social domination. A second, indirect but no less important advantage in rejecting racial identity while retaining unity in the struggle against oppression is the opening up of cultures to more people who are willing and able to appreciate them. The cultural heritage of black and nonblack Americans is neither singular nor exclusive. Our various cultures, like the various public discourses to which Toni Morrison calls our attention, are full of cross-references and complex influences among one another that cannot meaningfully be attributed or attached to any single group—or perhaps even separated. Attachments to cultures both change over time and vary among members of identifiable groups in a way that is belied by the common notion of racial identity carrying a cultural identity with it. Moreover, not only are societies and groups multicultural, but individuals are, too.[73] Color consciousness not only exposes the fiction of race but also recognizes that the cultural values that have been tied to the history of racial oppression are potentially open to all individuals, regardless of their color.

[73] I offer a more thorough defense along with evidence that supports this observation in "The Challenge of Multiculturalism in Political Ethics," *Philosophy and Public Affairs* 22, no. 3 (Summer 1993): 171–206.

But color consciousness shares with race consciousness one feature that some critics take to be as morally problematic as racial identity itself: the involuntary nature of the group identity. Although color consciousness does not carry a comprehensive cultural or political identity with it, it nonetheless imposes on us a group identity, whether or not we appreciate the identity attributed to us. Whether I like it or not, regardless of what I think or do or who I am in some more meaningful sense, I will be identified as white in this society. And other individuals will be identified as black. And so on. We can neither reflectively choose our color identity nor downplay its social significance simply by willing it to be unimportant. In these respects, our color consciousness is similar to our consciousness of language. We no more choose our color than choose the language by which we communicate with our fellow citizens. But our color no more binds us to send a predetermined group message to our fellow human beings than our language binds us to convey predetermined thoughts. Both color consciousness and linguistic consciousness offer us significant degrees of freedom to shape the messages that we send, even if we cannot escape the consciousness itself.[74]

An involuntary attribution of identity in itself therefore need not be terribly troubling: we are all identified by characteristics beyond our control, some of which—body build, for example—we may even wish were otherwise.[75] The fact that we are not free to choose our language is not cause for great moral concern. The involuntary attribution of a racial identity is morally troubling not simply, or primarily, because it is involuntary but for other reasons. It is a fiction parading or functioning as a scientific fact. It has the effect, often intended but even when not, of dividing

[74] Compare Benedict Anderson's thought-provoking discussion of nationality and its relationship to language in *Imagined Communities* (London: Verso, 1991).

[75] If we are not completely unfortunate, we will reflectively accept and appreciate many characteristics and affiliations that we are not free to choose. Our families and our citizenship are affiliations that we are typically not free to choose. When we reflectively accept the role of being our parents' children, for example, we also accept the obligations that attach to this role, ideally interpreting the obligations according to our own best moral lights. For an insightful discussion of reflective acceptance of role obligations, see Michael O. Hardimon, "Role Obligations," *Journal of Philosophy* 91 (July 1994): 333–63.

human beings against the cause of social justice. As long as the vast majority of Americans care little about racial injustice because they are not identified as black, and they therefore do less about it, racial identification serves to carry on the cause of racial injustice, undermining the constitutional right of all individuals to be treated as civic equals and obscuring our moral obligation to treat each other as equals. Treating people as members of different racial groups rather than as civic equals is another troubling consequence of race consciousness, which must also be challenged if we are effectively to address racial injustice.

Color consciousness is no more voluntaristic than race consciousness, but it is neither a fiction parading as fact nor as likely to divide us in the cause of social justice. By calling our attention to the superficiality of skin color (and facial features) as a continuing source of social differentiation, color consciousness helps expose in its very terminology the idea that race is a fiction and an ongoing source of social injustice. Yet color consciousness, for all its advantages over race consciousness, still raises some challenging questions, for example, about the obligations of black and nonblack Americans. Some critics who view race as a fiction nonetheless believe that black Americans, by virtue of their identity, have special obligations—to further the well-being of their oppressed group—that nonblack Americans do not have.

Do black Americans have special obligations? Are such obligations consistent with recognizing the obligations of all Americans, especially more economically and socially advantaged individuals, to do their part in responding to racial injustice? Should we be troubled by the fact that not all individuals reflectively accept such obligations to overcome racial injustice as consistent with their own self-understanding?[76]

One way of attributing special obligations to black Americans is parasitic on race consciousness. On this view, group membership is taken to be the primary source of individual obligations because it is somehow primordial, and greater obligations to fight racial injustice are therefore attributed to black Americans than to other Americans. This is the racial equivalent of the rich getting

[76] I am indebted here to the more extensive discussion of ethical identity in Appiah, "But Would That Still Be Me?" pp. 493–99.

richer and the poor getting poorer. Not only are more advantaged Americans largely let off the moral hook, black Americans who reflectively reject such special obligations are labeled unauthentic, false to their essential group identity as black Americans.

If we endorse only color consciousness, not race consciousness, then we must reject this conception of individual authenticity and the way in which it attributes special obligations to black Americans. This conception of authenticity imports the spurious idea of racial essence back into the idea of individual identity. Color consciousness, by contrast, faces up to the fact that Americans today are still identified by their color and treated in distinct, often morally indefensible ways by virtue of it. Not to be color conscious is not to face up to this fact. The color of Americans significantly affects their life chances and experiences, not for any essentialist reasons but for no less significant historical and social reasons, which no single individual is sufficiently powerful to change.

If we accept color consciousness as a facing up to these facts about what being black or white entails in our society, then we must begin not with any race-based or color-bound morality, but instead by associating color consciousness with a fundamentally color blind principle of obligation, based on fairness. (Fairness may not be the only defensible basis for conceiving of our social obligations, but it is the most commonly accepted basis and one that converges in its results with other conceptions of a color blind morality.) The principle, simply stated, is that everyone should do his or her fair share to overcome racial (as well as any other) injustice. This is a general obligation that applies to all individuals. Yet some special obligations for black *and* white Americans may flow from it. The special obligations of black Americans turn out to be different from, but by no means greater than, those of white Americans.

Faced with the troubling fact that other Americans are not doing their fair share, black Americans have long recognized the need to unite in order to combat racial injustice. (Members of other ascriptive groups have also recognized the need to unite to combat racial, ethnic, class, or gender injustices, but our focus here is solely on the special obligations generated by racial injustice directed toward black Americans.) Many of the public poli-

170

cies and individual practices that would effectively address racial injustice are collective goods: if they benefit some black Americans, they will in some significant way benefit (almost) all. Examples of such collective goods include affirmative action policies whose net effect is to reduce the racial stereotyping of high status jobs and to increase the civic standing of blacks. Examples of individual practices include pro bono legal and medical services rendered by black professionals to inner city communities that, in addition to helping less advantaged blacks, also help live down the stereotype of the black middle-class abandoning their brethren.[77] Not only do preferential hiring and pro bono work deliver individualized benefits to select people, they are also collective goods to the extent that they increase the general social standing of all black Americans. Particular examples of promising policies are less important than the general point: policies and practices that increase the social standing of black Americans as a group are likely to benefit almost all blacks as individuals because increasing the group's general status in society tends also to increase the opportunities of individual blacks (by decreasing the prejudicial denial of opportunities to individuals by virtue of their being identified as black).

This common, color blind ideal of fairness provides a basis for members of oppressed groups to criticize others who benefit from their efforts to combat racial injustice but who do nothing to aid the cause. But the same ideal of fairness frees individuals from being bound by the dominant group understanding of how the cause is best served. Doing one's share is not to be confused with playing the part that someone else has assumed the authority of assigning you. Responding to racial injustice is a matter of individuals acting in a way that they can reasonably defend as fair and consistent with their self-understandings. Fairness suggests that more advantaged blacks have greater obligations than less advantaged blacks, but not that they must fulfill their obligations in the way in which any majority—black or white—deems appropriate.

[77] For a far-ranging and insightful defense of a special obligation of black professionals to serve black communities, and the legal education appropriate to encourage such service, see David B. Wilkins, "Two Paths to the Mountaintop?" pp. 1981–2026.

There are multiple ways in which we all can identify with each other and reciprocate the beneficial acts of others. In fairness, none of us should be tied to the way chosen by others, provided that we too find a way to do our fair share.

Fairness also warns white Americans not to criticize from the sidelines. The fewer social burdens that individuals have been forced to bear, the greater the obligations are to combat racial injustice. Few of us come close to doing our fair share. My moral standing on this particular matter, like that of many other Americans, is suspect. I cannot realistically hope to do my fair share, but such a sobering recognition would be counterproductive were it to silence me from speaking out against racial injustices, or were it to paralyze and prevent any of us from trying to do something, however partial, to make the future of this country fairer to black Americans and better in moral terms for all Americans than the present.

There is another special obligation, which, like the special obligation of blacks, is color conscious even though it flows from the color blind ideal of fairness. White Americans (along with most other nonblack Americans) have a special obligation to fight racial injustice so as to decrease the likelihood that we will be the beneficiaries of unfair advantages that stem, for example, from the racial stereotyping of social offices and other forms of institutionalized injustices that unfairly disadvantage blacks. In addition to this special obligation to combat racial injustice, each of us also has general obligations which, as fairness suggests, increase in proportion to our individual capacity to help others.

Whatever our color or other group identification attributed to us, we are generally obligated to promote justice by virtue of what others have done (and are doing) to improve our lives and by virtue of our own capacity to help others. These general obligations increase in proportion to how much people have done to help us and how much we can do to help others. Fairness does not require that we fulfill our obligations by helping people of the same color, ethnicity, gender, or class of those who helped improve the conditions of our lives, assuming that we can figure out which group that was. Fairness obligates us to help disadvantaged individuals as we and others have been helped before, are being helped, and are capable of helping in the future (without undue sacrifice). The obligations of the average white American therefore are more demanding in absolute terms than those of the average black American. Similarly, the obligations of middle-class blacks are more demanding in absolute terms than those of less advantaged blacks.

What's right about color consciousness flows in this way from the truth in color blindness. The fundamental principle of justice as fairness is color blind. Its implications for public policy and the obligations of individuals, however, are not. Because our capacity, here and now, to help others without undue sacrifice varies by race (and class), the color blind principle of fairness leads to race consciousness (and class consciousness). To be committed to the color blind principle of fairness, therefore, entails a commitment to color consciousness but not to race consciousness.

Those of us who have unfairly benefited in the past, or will unfairly benefit in the future, if we do not act to change things, have special obligations, which flow from the general obligation to do our fair share to help others. We have these special obligations not because we asked to be unfairly advantaged but because we *have been* and *are* unfairly advantaged. Because being white has been a source of unfair benefits in this country, fairness generates special obligations that are color conscious.

Fairness also generates special obligations among black Americans, for historically contingent reasons. When some blacks go out of their way to improve the lot of all blacks, other blacks may become free-riders on these efforts if they do not either join the just cause or do something else, consistent with their own understanding of justice, to improve the lot of blacks (or less advantaged individuals). The source of this special obligation has nothing to do with an essentialist understanding of racial identity. It rests on the color blind ideal of fairness, which is also the general source of obligations for all individuals. Our obligations are on the whole greater to the extent that we are less oppressed.

Just as the color blind standard of fairness reveals what is right about color consciousness, so too what is right about color consciousness reveals the truth about color blindness. Color conscious obligations are contingently based on racial injustice. They do not derive from a notion of racial essence or authenticity, and they therefore stand opposed to the troubling kind of race consciousness that I discussed earlier.

I have suggested a principled way of recognizing the special obligations of black and white Americans without attributing the source of obligations ultimately to our group identity, and without losing sight of the general obligations of all individuals. The general principle is to help others who are disadvantaged, regardless of group identity. The special obligation of those who have benefited from racial injustice is to help undo the wrongs that perpetuate racial injustice. The special obligation of members of oppressed minorities is to do their fair share so they are not free-riders on the efforts of others who are at least as oppressed. Each of these obligations admits the moral freedom of every individual to interpret what justice demands in our nonideal world, and to act on that interpretation. We should give to others according to our capacity, and we should not be free-riders on the moral efforts of others. In this society, our identities as well as our obligations cannot help but be color conscious, but their source is the principle of fairness, which is color blind.[78]

Some critics may worry that color consciousness is too weak to do the work expected of it. Precisely because it is historically contingent in its self-understanding, color consciousness, these critics fear, exacts a high cultural price by rejecting any fundamental obligation of the form "First and foremost, perpetuate the culture of your own racial group." Will people who view their group identity as contingent rather than essential be as committed to carrying on the rich cultural tradition that has been historically connected to race consciousness on the part of blacks in the United States? Were color consciousness inconducive to perpetuating the rich cultures associated with black Americans, this would be an enormous loss not only to black Americans but to civilization and social life as we know it. The cultures associated with black Americans—consisting of customs, history, language, literature, music, and art—are an integral part of the cultural heritage of this

[78] For a pathbreaking discussion of obligations of minorities, which paves the way for this analysis, see Michael Walzer, "The Obligations of Oppressed Minorities," in *Obligations: Essays on Disobedience, War, and Citizenship* (Cambridge: Harvard University Press, 1970), pp. 46–73.

country. But the cultures change over time and they are not singular, they are plural, and they are not tied to any single group's identity.

Color consciousness is far more compatible with recognizing this vibrancy and plurality, along with the historical contingency, of the cultures associated with black Americans, than is race consciousness. To recognize the plurality and contingency of any community's cultures does nothing to diminish their value. Every major part of the cultural heritage of the United States is similarly changeable and contingent. And every major group's identity is culturally plural, not singular. Black and white Americans are multicultural. Moreover, the cultural heritage of black and white Americans are inseparable from each other and from every American's heritage. Many parts of our shared, pluralistic culture—jazz is one among many possible examples—are differentially valued by individuals, and differently connected to personal identities, but neither the value of jazz nor its survival depends on race consciousness or an essentialist view of group identity. Quite the contrary; once we recognize the historically contingent nature of color consciousness, we can look forward to a time—and help bring about the time—when the cultural experiences now primarily associated with black Americans are more widely appreciated and all cultural experiences are more broadly accessible because our society has become more openly and interactively multicultural than it is today.

What do I mean by a society becoming more openly and interactively multicultural? A society is openly multicultural to the extent that all individuals—depending on their appreciations and talents—have effective access to many cultural possibilities, no single one of which comprehensively defines any person's identity and all of which are subject to change by the creative efforts of individuals. A society is interactively multicultural to the extent that individuals experience the creative effects of the mingling of different cultures. A culture need not be universally or equally appreciated by all individuals to be valuable. But, other things being equal, cultures are more valuable to the extent that more people have access to them. This is a reason to look forward to the further decoupling of color and culture.

The disengagement of cultural affiliations from what Anthony

Appiah calls "too tightly scripted" identities would give all individuals, regardless of our color, far more scope to develop our talents and to enrich our lives with the cultural practices that we can reflectively appreciate.[79] Some of our cultural affiliations today—with jazz, for example—have already been disengaged from color consciousness. Color consciousness, by contrast, cannot be disengaged from the recognition of ongoing racial oppression and still retain its value. Were the struggle against racial injustice to succeed in this country, part of its success would be evidenced in the end of color consciousness and therefore the freeing of cultural identifications from any connection to race or color consciousness. Those cultural values that have grown up around race and color in this country would in all likelihood become far more fluid and subject to individually acknowledged affinities rather than socially ascribed identities.

Whereas race is a dangerous fiction and the value of color consciousness is contingent on the persistence of racial injustice, the cultural by-products of past and present struggles against racial injustice are enduringly valuable—although they will no doubt change over time with the creative efforts of individuals. Not only do they support present-day struggles to overcome racial justice—an important value in itself—but they also enrich individual lives with extraordinary expressions of human talent, imagination, and

---

[79] Compare Jorge L. A. Garcia, "African-American Perspectives, Cultural Relativism, and Normative Issues: Some Conceptual Questions," in *African-American Perspectives on Biomedical Ethics*, ed. Harley E. Flack and Edmund D. Pellegrino (Washington, D.C.: Georgetown University Press, 1992), p. 47: "A culture, however, must be the culture of some community and . . . communities exist only when people are tied one to another in common pursuits and a shared vision of what they wish to become." I am using culture in a more common and fluid but no less meaningful way here. Individuals who identify with most aspects of black American culture need not be (and generally are not) part of a single community whose members share a vision of what they wish to become. Rich and valuable cultures, including those associated as African-American, do not require a commitment to a particular "set of values, principles, or other beliefs," nor need they "constitute" their members' identities in any strong sense of the term (Garcia, "African-American Perspectives, Cultural Relativism, and Normative Issues," p. 28). Compare Anthony Appiah's discussion of culture in this volume.

historical experience, and with the ordinary pleasures of particularistic associations. These pleasures, like those of families, need not be equally accessible to be extremely valuable.

A Necessarily Incomplete Conclusion

The response to racial injustice that I have developed in this essay, although more inclusive than many, is still sorely incomplete. It reflects one person's inadequate efforts to chart a publicly justifiable course for addressing racial injustice by a multiplicity of means, only a few of which I could discuss in detail here. The political morality on which I base my response begins from where we now stand, in a society still beset by racial injustice, and looks for morally defensible ways of moving closer to a just society for all Americans. The color conscious policies that this political morality defends are based on a color blind principle of fairness, but I have argued, against advocates of color blind policies, that fairness in our society demands color consciousness (as well as class consciousness). What's right about color consciousness is also the truth about color blindness, and vice versa. Those (and only those) color conscious policies are justified that are both instrumentally valuable in overcoming racial injustice and consistent with counting all persons, whatever their skin color or ancestry, as civic equals.

When color conscious policies are no longer instrumental to overcoming racial injustice, our political morality should prepare us to leave these policies behind. Unlike affirmative action, which entails taking special steps to ensure nondiscrimination among all individuals, preferential treatment entails doing something regrettable (preferring a less qualified individual over a more qualified one) in order to do what may sometimes be on the whole right. This regret, in our social context, is not a sufficient reason for rejecting all policies of preferential treatment, let alone insisting that all our public policies be color blind. Were we to resort to color blindness in our public policies, we would not be able to pursue nondiscrimination in many situations, and therefore have far greater cause for regret. Without color conscious policies, we would not be acting in ways that benefit the least advantaged and that bring our society closer to the time when color blindness can be fair to everyone, regardless of color.

But color conscious policies are not nearly enough. We should embrace a multiplicity of means, including significant educational and economic reforms, such as making work pay and providing an adequate education for every child, that are not color conscious. We should also welcome the discovery of other policies—whether they be color blind or color conscious—that can bring us closer to a society in which color conscious policies will no longer be necessary.

The distinction between aspiration and accomplishment—which is central to Baldwin's recognition that "my inheritance was particular, specifically limited and limiting; [but] my birthright was vast, connecting me to all that lives, and to everyone, forever"—is also central to my defense of some color conscious policies. We are related to all human beings regardless of color, and we should seek liberty and equality not for some but for all. When we face up to our inheritance—of a society still beset by racial injustice—we find that some color conscious policies and some kinds of color consciousness may minimize injustice today and make it possible to be both fair and color blind in the future. This vision of the future is one that, despite our differences, we all can share.

Epilogue

*

K. ANTHONY APPIAH

> Because . . . racial inequality is the product of an unjust
> history, propagated across the generations in part by the
> segmented social structure of our race conscious society,
> it is appropriate that our government should be especially
> concerned when economic disparity takes a
> concentrated racial form.[1]

THERE IS a great deal of angry polemic about race in this country today. Accusations of racism, warranted and unwarranted, abound. *Rodney King, O.J. Simpson, welfare queens, quota queens, the bell curve*—each of these conjures debates with a distasteful tone. In this respect, discussions of race are perhaps typical, since, as many observers have noticed, public debate on many questions has developed an uncivil inflection.

In the academy, where race is the topic of discussion in almost every department of the humanities and the social sciences, controversies proliferate. We in the academy are sometimes angry, also; but even when we are not, we are adversarial, argumentative, disputatious. Our debates, too, can seem divided and divisive.

Perhaps it is time to point to some common ground.

Amy Gutmann has defended eloquently the reasonable answer to the question, Why should the government not be color blind? The reasonable answer is that the government *can't* be color

---

[1] Glenn C. Loury *One by One from the Inside Out* (New York: Free Press, 1995) p. 102. My epigraph is preceded by these words: "Due to slavery and racial caste, there has come into existence a distinct, insular, subgroup of our society that began with severe disadvantages (in comparison to others) in the endowments of wealth, experience, and reputation so crucial to economic success. The social structural point is that for as long as one can foresee, and without regard to legal prohibitions against discrimination in formal contract, we may confidently predict the practice of informal social discrimination—that is

blind because society isn't—people and institutions treat citizens differently according to whether they are black or white, yellow or brown—and this fact raises questions of fairness. The quotation that serves as my epigraph is from Glen Loury, one of the best-known black conservative intellectuals in America today. I am sure that Loury would not agree with everything in Amy Gutmann's essay, or in mine. But on this fundamental point, all three of us would agree. In the contemporary United States, this basic principle is no longer radical. Not only is Professor Gutmann's starting point reasonable, it is widely accepted.

The reason, I think, that the view that there is a role for government in protecting racial minorities from present discrimination (as well as the persisting results of discrimination in the past) is such a mainstream belief is that, despite the current unpopularity of the word "liberal," the basic propositions of modern liberalism are extremely widely accepted in this country today.

What I mean by "modern liberalism" is the product of the New Deal, when liberals added to their stock-in-trade of concern for liberty and the government's respect for individual rights, a commitment to state guarantees of the basic economic welfare of each citizen.[2] Just as the liberal insistence on rights is no longer politically controversial—conservative Republicans support the Bill of Rights just as avidly as liberal Democrats—so the fundamental notion that the government must play a role in assuring basic economic welfare and securing fairness in the private economy is also pretty widely shared. Who is seriously opposed to antidiscrimination laws in employment or to the persistence of the protections provided by Social Security, Medicare, and Medicaid?[3]

---

discrimination in choice of social affiliation, which occurs along these group lines. This practice of discrimination in the social sphere implies the continuing inequality of opportunity in the economic sphere."

[2] This consensus in Europe is known, of course, as social democracy.

[3] Actually, of course, there are serious people who hold these views; but they're intellectually radical conservative academics, with little following outside the academy. Richard Epstein is against antidiscrimination law, for example: see *Forbidden Grounds: The Case against Employment Discrimination Laws* (Cambridge: Harvard University Press, 1992). And Thomas Sowell seems sometimes to be against welfare provision, though largely on the grounds that it is bad for its recipients: see "A vicious vision," *Forbes Magazine*, July 31, 1995, p. 57.

There is, of course, substantial disagreement about how to implement these two strands of liberalism: commitment to rights underlies both many pro-life and most pro-choice positions; and there is, as we all know only too well, active debate about what level of welfare and health provision defines the minimum acceptable guarantee that America should offer those who live here. But it is important to stress how much these debates occur within a consensus that has deep and deepening roots in American political traditions.

Similarly, I believe, the recognition of the sovereignty of the individual, which underlies much of the argument of my own essay, is nourished by the wellspring of an American individualism; tempered by an equally American conviction that individuals flourish only within families, churches and temples, communities and professions, as private people as well as political citizens. Americans value private life, private choice, and a wide sphere of freedom from the dictates of government; but anarchism—the view that government is inherently evil—has not flourished here. Even the current upsurge of hostility to politics and to politicians does not run against this basic historical conviction: it is not government but bad government (and bad governors) that has made people skeptical. So Americans balance individual interest and the demands of many forms of community, they seek an equilibrium between private life and public citizenship.

I want, in closing, to draw the reader's attention to another American tradition—one with roots in the Enlightenment vision of many of the American founders—that also underlies these essays. That tradition is a commitment to reasoned debate among citizen equals as the way forward, combined with an optimism about democracy's capacity to face the challenges that are constantly raised in the difficult business of sharing our streets, our towns, our states, our country, and this small planet.

Race has been a great challenge to the hope of reason and the spirit of democracy from the beginning of the American republic. Thomas Jefferson, as I pointed out in my essay, saw from the beginning that black slavery was incompatible with the best principles of the American revolution; and he worried too, in a passage I cited, about the political consequences of the "deep rooted prejudices entertained" by many of his white fellow citizens. But Jefferson had, of course, enormous hope for his young nation. Even in the worst of times, some black Americans have kept their vision and their hope. Two months after the Dred Scott decision, Frederick Douglass told the American Anti-Slavery Society in New York: "As a man, an American, a citizen, a colored man of both Anglo-Saxon and African descent, I denounce this representation as a most scandalous and devilish perversion of the Constitution."[4] It is not just in the name of his humanity but also by virtue of his American citizenship that Douglass assaults slavery and its legal defenders; and his faith is in the fundamental justice of the American Constitution.

Because Amy Gutmann and I are both passionate democrats, we believe deeply in the importance of reasonable public debate about the problems and the possibilities that face this nation. Much of what is written and spoken about race in our current debates is dishonest, confused, ill-informed, unhelpful. As the reader already knows, if he or she has read this far, this book does not offer answers to all or even most of the problems of race that confront Americans today. But it does, we hope, contribute some tools for thinking about those problems and some context for reflecting on them: and it seeks to do so candidly, clearly, and in the light of our own explorations of racial reality in America yesterday and today. We hope, in short, to contribute to the discourse of a great nation facing the challenge of living up to its best principles.[5]

At the beginning of this century, W.E.B. Du Bois wrote with characteristic vigor and, alas, with continuing pertinence:

[4] *The Life and Writings of Frederick Douglass*, vol. 2: *Pre–Civil War Decade*, ed. Philip S. Foner (New York: International Publishers, 1950).

[5] Talk of America's best principles here does not mean that we should forget that the history of black disenfranchisement has an equal claim to be an American tradition, reflecting one of this country's less admirable traditions. Part of the history to which Amy Gutmann adverts when she points to the benefits of whiteness is the consistent incorporation of European immigrants *as whites*. See David R. Roediger, *The Wages of Whiteness: Race and the Making of the American Working Class* (London: Verso, 1991).

Strange, is it not, my brothers, how often in America those great watchwords of human energy—"Be strong!" "Know thyself!" "Hitch your wagon to a star!"—how often these die away into dim whispers when we face these seething millions of black men? And yet do they not belong to them? . . . Are you afraid to let them try? Fear rather, in our common fatherland, lest we live to lose those great watchwords of liberty and opportunity which yonder in the eternal hills their fathers fought with your fathers to preserve.[6]

Jefferson, in the eighteenth century, Douglass, in the nineteenth, Du Bois in the twentieth: it is, as Amy Gutmann has so rightly insisted, the task of citizens of every color to play their part in America's long conversation about race.

[6] *The Colored American Magazine*, May 1904; reprinted in *W.E.B. Du Bois Speaks*, ed. Philip S. Foner (New York: Pathfinder Press, 1970), p. 141.

* Index *

admissions policies: class conscious policies and, 139–47; color blind policies and, 16–17, 126–27

affirmative action: at AT&T, 135–36, 137–38; benefits of, 134n, 171; deliberative democracy and, 150–51; justifications for, 16–18; moral arguments, political leadership and, 13, 150–51; Piscataway, New Jersey, case, 10–12, 118–19, 126–30; versus preferential treatment, 130–31, 177; *The Scar of Race* study on, 148–51; at University of California, 16–17; white Americans' responses to, 148–50. *See also* class conscious policies; color blind policies

"African-American Perspectives, Cultural Relativism, and Normative Issues" (Garcia), 176n

African-Americans: African-American identity, 95–96; class differences among, 26–27; culture of, 22–24, 88, 89–90, 95–96; Jefferson on the apparent inferiority of, 43–47, 76; life scripts of, 98–99; middle-class African-Americans, 24–27; moral obligations of, 170–74; segregation of, 26

Alland, Garland, 61–62n

Anderson, Benedict, 168n

Anscombe, Elizabeth, 78

Appiah, Anthony: Gutmann on, 116, 176; Wilkins on, 4–9, 16, 18–19, 21, 23–24

Arnold, Matthew, 52–61; on Celtic versus Briton racial character, 52–54; on culture, 90–91, 96, 102–3, 104; *Culture and Anarchy*, 58–59, 60, 64, 90–91; versus Darwin, 67–68; and literary racialism, 62, 63, 64; on the mixture of racial essences, 56–61; *On the Study of Celtic Literature*, 52–58, 59, 60, 64; and racial

versus environmental influences, 60–61; as a racialist, 54–56, 59–61, 67–68, 76

Ashe, Arthur, 106, 137

Asian-Americans, 28

AT&T Model Plan, 135–36, 137–38

authenticity: and identity, 93–96, 98; and the moral obligations of African-Americans, 170

Autobiography (Jefferson), 42–43, 52

Baldwin, James, 106, 178

Banneker, Benjamin, 46–47, 51–52

Battle of the Books (Swift), 91

Being and Nothingness (Sartre), 78–79

Beitz, Charles, 156n, 157n

The Bell Curve (Murray and Herrnstein), 71–72, 99–100, 117n

Bickel, Alexander, 119

biology: biological concepts of race, 67–71, 72–74; genetics and race, 66, 68, 69–73, 113–18

Blum, Larry, 89n

Brest, Paul, 132n

Bronsted, Johnnes Nicolaus, 39n

Bush v. Vera, 158n

California Civil Rights Initiative, 136–37

capitalism, 100–102

Carlyle, Thomas, 62

Carroll, Joseph, 61n

causal theory of reference, 39–41

Cavalli-Sforza, L. Luca, 116n

civilization, versus culture, 84–85

class: class consciousness versus race consciousness, 12–13, 24–27; class differences among African-Americans, 26–27

class conscious policies, 111–12, 138–51; "class, not race" arguments, 111, 138–43; versus class *and* color policies, 112, 143–47; middle-class African-Americans

185

Swain, Carol M., 134n, 139n, 155n, 156n
Swift, Jonathan, 91

Taine, Hippolyte, 63–64
Tamir, Yael, 165n
Tay Sachs Disease, 117
Taylor, Charles, 92–95, 98
Thernstron, Abigail, 154n
Thompson, Dennis, 126n, 127n, 135n
Tractatus Logico-Philosophicus (Wittgenstein), 32–33
traditional societies, 85–86
Trilling, Lionel, 93n

United States, culture in, 86–88
Updergrave, Walter, 25n
unity, identity and, 104–5
university admissions: class conscious policies and, 139–47; color blind policies and, 127
University of California, affirmative action at, 16–17
U.S. Constitution: as color blind, 3–4, 11; Fourteenth Amendment, 139n
U.S. Supreme Court cases: *Bush v. Vera*, 158; *Miller v. Johnson*, 159–61; overview of, 13; *Plessy v. Ferguson*, 3, 77, 118n; *Shaw v. Hunt*, 152n, 158n; *Shaw v. Reno*, 152–53, 159, 161n; *Wygant v. Jackson Board of Education*, 132n

vague criterial theory, 36–38
voting power, 156–58, 159–60
Voting Rights Act of 1965 and Voting Rights Amendments of 1982, 158n

Walzer, Michael, 119n, 121n, 136n, 145n, 174n
Waters, Mary, 80n
Weismann, August, 61n
white Americans: culture among white American women, 89; moral obligations of, 170–74; responses to affirmative action, 148–50
White Women, Race Matters: The Social Construction of Whiteness (Frankenberg), 89
Wilde, Oscar, 96
Wilkins, David, 89n, 163, 171n
Wills, Christopher, 116n
Wilson, William Julius, 24, 125n, 147n
Wittgenstein, Ludwig, 32–33, 36
Wong, David, 89n
Wright, Lawrence, 115n
Wygant v. Jackson Board of Education, 132n

Young, Iris Marion, 162–63n
Young, Michael, 139n

Zack, Naomi, 37n

ABOUT THE AUTHORS

K. ANTHONY APPIAH is Professor of Afro-American Studies and Philosophy at Harvard University. His books include *In My Father's House: Africa in the Philosophy of Culture* (Oxford), which received the Annisfield-Wolf Award and the Herskovits Award of the African Studies Association for the best work published in English on Africa.

AMY GUTMANN is Laurance S. Rockefeller University Professor of Politics and Dean of the Faculty at Princeton University. She was the founding director of the University Center for Human Values and is the author of many books, including *Democratic Education* (Princeton), *Liberal Equality* (Cambridge), and, most recently, *Democracy and Disagreement* (Harvard), with Dennis Thompson.

DAVID B. WILKINS is Professor of Law and Director of the Program on the Legal Profession at Harvard Law School. He is the author of many articles on legal ethics, legal education, and the role of race in personal and professional identity. He is currently working on a book about black lawyers in corporate law practice.